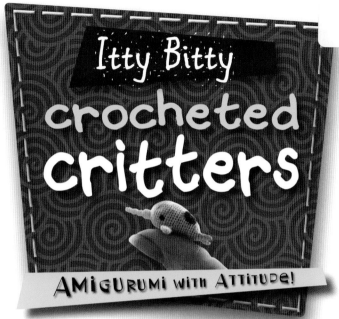

Itty Bitty crocheted critters

AMIGURUMI WITH ATTITUDE!

erin clark

TUTTLE Publishing

Tokyo | Rutland, Vermont | Singapore

Published by Tuttle Publishing, an imprint of Periplus Editions (HK) Ltd.

www.tuttlepublishing.com

Copyright © 2013 Erin Clark

Library of Congress Cataloging-in-Publication Data in Process

ISBN 978-4-8053-1251-3

Distributed by

North America, Latin America & Europe
Tuttle Publishing
364 Innovation Drive, North Clarendon, VT 05759-9436 U.S.A.
Tel: 1 (802) 773-8930; Fax: 1 (802) 773-6993
info@tuttlepublishing.com; www.tuttlepublishing.com

Asia Pacific
Berkeley Books Pte Ltd
61 Tai Seng Avenue #02-12, Singapore 534167.
Tel: (65) 6280-1330; Fax: (65) 6280-6290
inquiries@periplus.com.sg; www.periplus.com

Japan
Tuttle Publishing
Yaekari Building, 3rd Floor, 5-4-12 Osaki, Shinagawa-ku, Tokyo 141 0032.
Tel: (81) 3 5437-0171; Fax: (81) 3 5437-0755
sales@tuttle.co.jp; www.tuttle.co.jp

First edition
17 16 15 14 13   5 4 3 2 1   1307EP
Printed in Hong Kong

The Tuttle Story: "Books to Span the East and West"

Many people are surprised to learn that the world's largest publisher of books on Asia had its humble beginnings in the tiny American state of Vermont. The company's founder, Charles E. Tuttle, belonged to a New England family steeped in publishing.

Immediately after WW II, Tuttle served in Tokyo under General Douglas MacArthur and was tasked with reviving the Japanese publishing industry. He later founded the Charles E. Tuttle Publishing Company, which thrives today as one of the world's leading independent publishers.

Though a westerner, Tuttle was hugely instrumental in bringing a knowledge of Japan and Asia to a world hungry for information about the East. By the time of his death in 1993, Tuttle had published over 6,000 books on Asian culture, history and art—a legacy honored by the Japanese emperor with the "Order of the Sacred Treasure," the highest tribute Japan can bestow upon a non-Japanese.

With a backlist of 1,500 titles, Tuttle Publishing is more active today than at any time in its past—inspired by Charles Tuttle's core mission to publish fine books to span the East and West and provide a greater understanding of each.

Contents

Introduction

Hello and welcome! I'm back to bring you more cute critters, made exponentially cuter by crocheting them in miniature. You can make most any pattern in miniature simply by shrinking your supplies. Likewise all of the patterns in this book can be made full sized by swapping out the floss for worsted weight yarn and moving up to an H hook.

What use could you have for tiny crochet you ask? You can use them in a sculpture piece, for doll houses or for display on their own. I mean really, they are pretty darn cute. You can also use them to make decorative fiber terrariums, directions and ideas for which you will also find later in the book.

So grab some magnifiers and good bright lamp and let's get started on some minigurmi.

—*Voodoo Maggie*

BASIC STITCHES

These instructions assume a knowledge of how begin a chain and offers all the stitches you will need to finish the patterns in this book.

SINGLE CROCHET (SC)

Insert your hook into stitch or chain yarn over and pull through work. Yarn over again and pull through both loops on hook. Continue on in this manner for as many stiches as indicated in pattern.

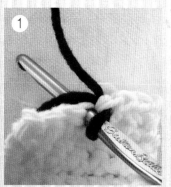

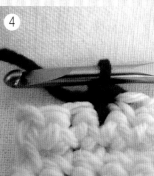

HALF DOUBLE CROCHET (HDC)

Yarn over and insert your hook into stitch, yarn over and pull through work. Yarn over and pull through all three loops on hook.

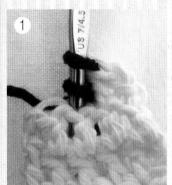

DOUBLE CROCHET (DC)

Yarn over and insert hook into stitch, yarn over and pull through work. Yarn over and pull through two loops on hook. Yarn over and pull through remaining two loops.

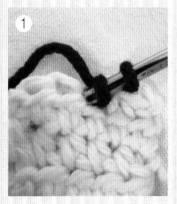

DECREASING AND INCREASING

Standard Decreasing is best for flat pieces that will be visible from both sides.
   To decrease you insert your hook into first of stitches to be decreased, yarn over and pull through. Repeat for remainder of stitches to be decreased.
   Yarn over and pull through all loops on hook.

 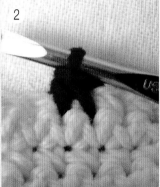  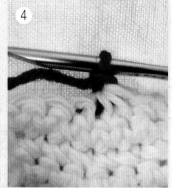

Invisible Decreasing is best for working in the round when the back of the piece will not be visible.
   To work the invisible decrease you insert your hook into the front loop of the first of stitches to be decreased, do not yarn over, insert hook into next front loop.
   Yarn over and pull through all front loops. Yarn over and pull through the two loops on hook.
   The photos below are examples.

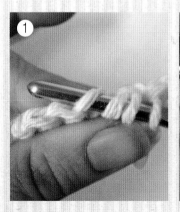 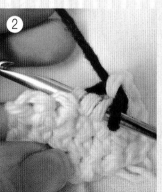  

Increasing is simple technique where you crochet multiple stitches into one stitch space
The below photos are examples.

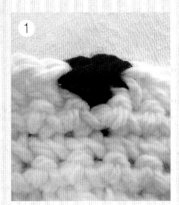

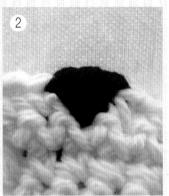

optional tools

FELTING NEEDLE: For stuffing and shaping the small pieces. Stuffing is rather springy by nature and using the felting needle gives a dense body that will hold it's shape with regular handling.

A SMALL BLUNT TIP OBJECT: I like to use the non business end of a bamboo skewer. If you don't have one you can use your scissors and open them up just a bit. The ends will grab the stuffing and help compact it, but it won't be as snug as using the felting needle. If you haven't got anything else the non hook end of a crochet will do.

PLIERS: in case your needle gets stuck in a tight stitch, pulling it through with your hands can be difficult and lead to a smooshed or dirty final piece. Just remember not to pull too hard or you could snap the needle in half.

Tools and materials

GOOD SHARP SCISSORS: preferably no longer than 3-4 inches. Larger scissors get cumbersome when working with your tiny pieces.

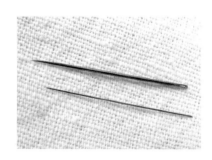

EMBROIDERY NEEDLE: long and thin needles will work the best for weaving in yarn ends, it makes pulling through the tiny tight stitches a good deal easier. Make sure the eye isn't too wide or sewing up your mini will be a very tough and leave your piece looking like Swiss cheese.

SMALL CROCHET HOOKS: Size 8-10 for double stranded, size 10-12 for single strand. You can use any size if you adjust your fiber accordingly. All these miniatures can be made full sized buy using a G-H hook and a worsted weight yarn.

STUFFING: For stuffing your creations. I prefer to use a cotton or cotton-poly blend, it holds it shape better than straight poly-fill.

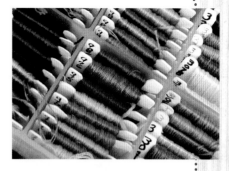

CROSS STITCH FLOSS OR CROCHET THREAD: I prefer DMC personally and will include the color number for DMC skeins, and total number of skeins used in all the patterns in this book.

ITEMS THAT CAN BE USED FOR EYES: You can use French knots, a triple strand will stand out the best. Small beads are great, even small brads might work depending on the size of your finished piece and the look you are going for.

CROCHETING IN THE ROUND

 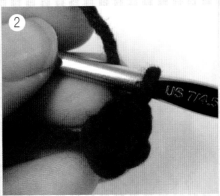 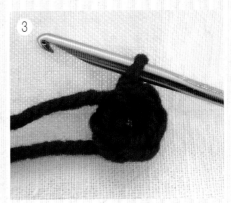

Crocheting in the round is very easy once you learn the ropes. There are several ways to start your circle, but for this book I'm going to show you the one I use.

Begin by chaining 2, Single crochet 6 (or eight depending on pattern) into the first chain you made. Do not finish or slip stitch, simply start the next round in the first stitch of previous row. You'll double your stitches on the next row by crocheting two into each stitch.

For subsequent rows you'll add one single crochet between the 2SC stitches. The photos below show examples of ever increasing rows.

CHANGING COLORS AND JOINING NEW YARN

There are three main reasons to join new yarn to your project:

THE FIRST: A color change at the end of a row. When you reach the end of your row, yarn over with the new yarn and pull through the loop on hook. Continue on with your pattern.

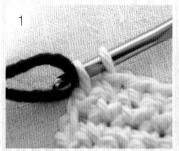

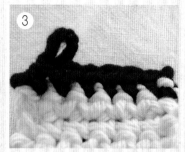

THE SECOND: A color change in the middle of your project. When working the last stitch before a color change, yarn over for the final time with the new color and pull through the remaining loops of previous color. This will give you a smoother change

THE THIRD: Running of yarn mid project. Insert your hook into next stitch, yarn over with new yarn and pull through. Yarn over and pull through both loops on hook. Continue on with your pattern.

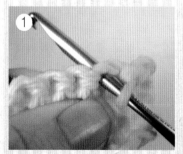

STUFFING YOUR PIECES

It is very important to keep the shape of the finished piece in mind when stuffing. You can't just cram your pieces full of stuffing and expect them to turn out correctly.

Take the photos to the left for example. The one on the far left is what the finished piece should look like. The one on the right is what happens when you stuff the piece to full capacity without regard to the shape. That is why there are reference photos for each individual piece of the patterns, so you can replicate the finished plushies as closely as possible.

It is also very important not to over stuff, crochet will stretch and leave gaps between the stitches and the stuffing will show.

FINISHING YOUR PIECES

SC ALL TOGETHER

This method only works well if you have ten or less final stitches in your last row. Two hooks are needed for this technique. To work it you put the first hook through the front loops only of half your stitches.

Then using the second hook (the first is still in your piece) repeat the process for the remaining stitches.

When you've reached the end, yarn over and pull through all loops on your hook. Remove working loop from hook and transfer to waiting hook.

Pull through the remaining stitches and pull through. Work a chain or two and pull thread all the way through the stitch

SEWING IN THE FRONT LOOPS

This method is the cleanest I've seen, and creates a finish that nearly mimics the beginning of your piece. When you reach the end of your piece and pull the thread all the way through the stitch. Take the tail and thread a needle. Run the needle under the first loop of each stitch like a whip stitch.

FINISHING OFF

When you finish off for the purposes of this book, you simply work a chain (or two if you like) after you last stitch and then pull thread all the way through the stitch. This creates a knot to keep your piece from unraveling.

other tips and tricks

For the purposes of this book only all rows are worked by turning the piece at the end of the row, and all rounds are worked in a continuous loop.

Joining with a single crochet: Secure your yarn to your hook insert into stitch yarn over and pull through work. Yarn over and pull through both loops. If your pattern calls for you to join with a double crochet, yarn over before you insert you hook into stitch and work like you would a regular double crochet

When I finish a piece that is going to be sewn to the body of a plush, I like to leave a tail long enough to sew it with. Using the tail eliminates a few extra ends to weave and makes the piece a little more secure. This is especially handy with miniatures as you can use the length of thread to sew your finished piece into a terrarium scene.

When sewing your pieces together don't sew straight up and down, it will leave a very noticeable seam. Instead sew on a diagonal across the stitch to make the seam invisible.

If you're sewing on a piece that needs to be symmetrical, it is very helpful to pin the piece in place with straight pins. But keep an eye out not to snag your yarn.

If you forget to place your safety eyes before you finished the piece (I do it a lot), you can remedy the problem by using fabric glue and gluing the eyes onto the piece. *Note do not do this if you are making the toy for a child, safety eyes are the safest way to go for children's toys. With miniatures this is not really an issue as you will most likely be using beads or French knots for eyes.

THINGS TO KEEP IN MIND

1. Always, always have clean dry hands. The floss will pick up any dirt or oils on your fingers. Likewise wet floss will pick up any dirt or grime on your hands and leave you with a streaky finished piece

*A good way to spot clean a miniature is to use a q-tip and a bit of peroxide. Soak the q-tip with the peroxide and dab it on the dirty portion of your piece. Do not scrub just let it bubble and dry on it's own. Test your thread first to make sure it won't bleach out.

2. Good lighting is key. Working with the small stitches will result in eyestrain, give yourself the best lighting you can to make it easier on yourself.

3. Keep your projects away from furry pets! Pet hair in a mini is a nightmare.

4. Have patience. It's going to be tough starting out the new pieces, the thread is tiny and if your stitches are tight you're going to end up having to undo and redo the beginning rows, possibly more than once. It's just part and parcel of crocheting on a smaller scale.

5. Hook size is very important. You need a hook that will give you a good size stitch for the thread you are using, if the hook is too small the stitches will be too tight and your finished piece will be stiff and full of puckers. Not to mention working on it will be difficult and frustrating.

6. You might want a thimble. I poke myself on a regular basis with the tiny hooks. They are small, metal and sharp, just like a needle and I frequently find myself bleeding and tender after working on a miniature.

7. If you are working with multiple strands of floss, be careful not to cross them into a stitch. They can get caught up in knots that won't pull out easily if at all.

8. When you are weaving in your ends, and you've pulled the thread back out the fabric, cut it as close to the body of the work as possible without cutting into your thread. Then just insert your sewing needle into the body nearby and run the tip of it under where the thread is showing and it will snag it and pull it into the body.

HOW TO WORK A FRENCH KNOT

Insert your threaded needle into your piece, having it come out where you want your knot to be.

Hold your thread with your left hand (or right if you're a lefty) and wrap it around your needle from above the needle.

The more you wrap the larger your finished knot will be, be keep in mind it's all being held in place with one small stitch. So too many loops on the needle will result in a sloppy knot.

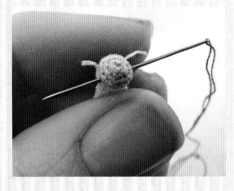

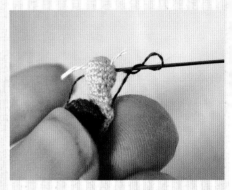

When you've got your desired amount of loops on your needle, insert it back into your piece near where it comes up but not in the same hole.

Pull your thread snug against needle with pulling too tight. Hold onto loops as you pull your needle and thread through the piece.

Tie off or weave in end as you prefer.

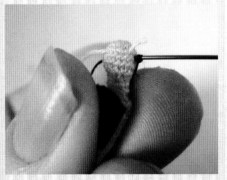

The Basics of Picking Your Container

There are very few limitations on what sort of container you can use for a terrarium, so what you'll be looking for is something that will show off the scene you have planned.

You'll want to avoid colored or milky glass. Make sure that if there is a pattern or writing on it that it won't obscure the view of your miniature creations.

You'll need to also take the opening of the container into consideration. If you have a narrow necked bottle, you'll only be able to get smaller or thinner pieces into it. This will affect not only the materials used but how it's finished.

For example if you use a wide mouth container you can sew all the pieces together outside of the container and just insert the finished piece into the jar.

With a narrow bottle you'll need to insert the base layers in individually and glue them into place. You might have to do the same with the feature pieces.

BASE LAYERS

All your terrariums will vary depending on many different factors, such as the size and shape of your jar, your available materials and of course you vision for finished product.

With a few basic elements you can create a variety of terrariums.

The first thing you'll need is the layers that are the foundation your miniatures will sit on.

If you are going for a realistic look then you'll want to do one or two layers in black or very dark grey, a few layers in a dark brown, then one or two more in green if you want to skip the step with the felting needle. You can of course change that up any way you like to suit your piece.

To start your layer pieces use this:

FOUNDATION: Ch 2, SC 6 in second Ch from hook

ROUND 1. *2SC in each* around

From here it will depend on how large your container is, just continue adding rounds and increasing the number of single crochets between 2SC stitches. Like so:

ROUND 2. *SC 1, 2SC in next* around

ROUND 3. *SC 2, 2SC in next* around, and so on add on stitch between each 2SC until you reach the desired size.

One of the great things about the terrariums is that you don't have to work a whole round if you don't need it. Say your layer is too small after four rows but too big after five, just work the next row a few stitches at a time until it fits how you want it to in the jar and finish it off when you get there.

Making a Terrarium

Not all containers are going to be round, for example the one used in this terrarium.

To make the layers for this piece, I chained until it was one stitch shy of being the length of the container, then just singled crocheted in rows until it was one row shy of filling the depth. Then crochet around all the edges with a Chain for each corner.

You can work your layers in any fiber you want, you could even just cut squares of felt if you prefer.

I like to use medium weight yarn, it works up faster and gives a nice finished texture.

If you choose to use thread or floss, keep in mind that you will need to work bigger layers and more of them to fill your container.

If you use chunky yarn the layer will work up even faster but be even thicker.

Using a combination of fibers can create some lovely texture.

Making Greenery and Small Flowers

Adding moss can be as simple as adding a few layers crocheted in green yarn or again, cutting it out of felt. If you want to add a little more depth and texture you can shred either bits of felt or yarn in various shades to make fluff. This fluff can be sewn or needle felted into the top layer of your base.

After you get the moss layer finished you can add more detail by creating French Knots over your base. You can create many in clusters of varying colors or a random scattering of just a solid color.

You can use yarn, thread or even ribbon to create different sized knots.

You can crochet some vines also. (Best if done with thread, not yarn)

Vines

FOUNDATION: {Ch 5, SC in third Ch from hook, Ch 1, Skip 1, SC 1, Ch between 8 an 11} repeat as many times as you need to until your vine has reached desired length.
For some small cup flowers; You need one strand, approximately 20 inches long

Simple Flowers

FOUNDATION: Ch 2, SC 5 in second Ch from hook
ROUND 1. *2SC in each* around
ROUND 2. *SC 1, 2SC in next* around
ROUNDS 3-4. SC around
Finish off.

For some added detail add a few French Knots to the inside of the flower in a contrasting color.

Cone Shape for Trees or Bushes

FOUNDATION: Ch 2, SC 6 in second hook
ROUND 1. SC around
ROUND 2. *2SC in each* around
ROUNDS 3-4. SC around
ROUND 5. *SC 1, 2SC in next* around
ROUNDS 6- DESIRED HEIGHT. SC around

Making Mushrooms

I love cute little mushrooms and they look great in a terrarium. Here are a few ways I like to make mushrooms.

You can use a nice thick French Knot in a bold color, then using a cream or tan, come up underneath the knot and work several half hitch knots around the anchoring threads until you it looks like a good stem length.

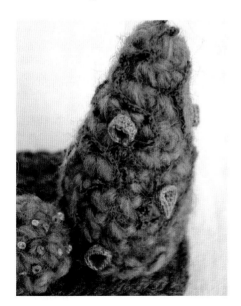

Half Hitch Knot

Small Cap Mushrooms

Cap

FOUNDATION: Ch 2, SC 6
ROUND 1. *2SC in each* around
ROUND 2. *SC 1, 2SC in next* around
ROUND 3. *SC 2, 2SC in next* around
ROUND 4. *SC 3, 2SC in next* around
ROUND 5. SC around
ROUND 6. *SC 4, 2SC in next*

Flat or Upturned Mushroom

FOUNDATION: Ch 2, SC 7
ROUND 1. *2SC in each* around
ROUND 2. *SC 1, 2SC in next* around
ROUND 3. *SC 2, 2SC in next* around
ROUND 4. *SC 3, 2SC in next* around
ROUND 5. *SC 4, 2SC in next* around
ROUND 6. {SC 5, 2SC in next} four times, SC 18
ROUND 7. SC 6, finish off

Stem

FOUNDATION: Ch 2, SC 6
ROUND 1. *2SC in each* around
ROUND 2. SC in back loop only
ROUND 3. SC around
ROUND 4. 2SCtog, SC 4
ROUND 5. 2SCtog, SC 3
ROUNDS 6. however long you want the stem. SC around.

Finishing Your Terrarium

If you are using a long bottle, you can use a bamboo skewer to push into place

Wide Mouth Jar

Stack your base layers and sew them all together but the top, this will be the moss layer.

Try not to sew them too tight or they will bubble up in the center.

Take your top layer and add moss, French Knots and mushrooms. Sew your main pieces into place.

Add your moss layer to the stack and sew in place.

Insert finished stack into jar, if you want it to be permanent add a few drops of tacky glue first.

Narrow Mouth Jar

If gluing into place, add a few drops to bottom of container

Add the base layers one at a time with a few drops of glue in between each.

Add your small details, like moss and French Knots.

Roll layers to insert them into bottle and use bamboo skewer to help unroll and push into place. If you want to make sure to not get glue on the finished side of your piece you can use two skewers. One to hold the piece up and the other to dab glue onto the piece.

Glue on larger details, again using two skewers can be very helpful for this

Finishing the Terrarium

If you'd like to hang something from the top of the container, I recommend using a cork and attaching whatever it is that you'd like to hang with a small, flat head straight pin.

You can also add interest to the outside of the terrarium by adding additional small details.

Leaves

FOUNDATION: Ch 2, SC 6 in second Ch from hook. 6
ROUND 1. *2SC in each* around. 12
ROUND 2. *SC 1, 2SC in next* around. 18
ROUND 3. SC 2, HDC, 2DC, Ch 1, 2DC, SC 6. 14 (finish before row ends)
Finish off.

Abbreviations

SC: Single Crochet
2SC: Single Crochet twice in same stitch
2SCTOG: Single Crochet two stitches together, or decrease
3DC: Double Crochet three times
SS: Slip Stitch
JWSC: Join with Single Crochet
**: Repeat indicated directions across row
{}: Directions in brackets will be repeated a specified number of times

Materials

Skeins of DMC #700 for of body.
Less than 1 skein of DMC #3328 for Jaw insert
Less than 1 skein of DMC White for teeth
Size 10 crochet hook for double stand
Size 12 crochet hook for single strand.
Small to medium black beads for eyes.**
Sewing needle

Tail and Body

FOUNDATION: Ch 2, SC 6 in second hook from Ch. 6
ROUND 1. 2SC, SC 5. 7
ROUND 2. SC around. 7
ROUND 3. 2SC, SC 6. 8
ROUND 4. SC around. 8
ROUND 5. 2SC, SC 7. 9
ROUND 6. SC around. 9
ROUND 7. 2SC, SC 8. 10
ROUND 8. SC around. 10
ROUND 9. 2SC, SC 4, 2SC, SC 4. 12

ROUND 10. 2SC, SC 5, 2SC, SC 5. 14

ROUNDS 11-13. SC around. 14

ROUND 14. 2SC, SC 6, 2SC, SC 6. 16

ROUNDS 15-16. SC around. 16

ROUND 17. 2SC, SC 7, 2SC, SC 7. 18

ROUNDS 18-19. SC around. 18

ROUND 20. 2SC, SC 8, 2SC, SC 8. 20

ROUND 21. 2SC, SC 9, 2SC, SC 9. 22.

ROUNDS 22-23. SC around. 22

ROUND 24. *SC 5, 2SC in next* around. 26

ROUND 25. *SC 6, 2SC in next* around. 30

ROUND 26. *SC 7, 2SC in next* around. 34

ROUND 27. SC around. 34

ROUND 28. *SC 8, 2SC in next* around. 38

ROUNDS 29-30. SC around. 38

ROUND 31. *SC 9, 2SC in next* around. 42

ROUNDS 32-40. SC around. 42

ROUND 41. *SC 9, 2SCtog* around. 38

ROUNDS 42-45. SC around. 38

ROUND 46. SC 19, {2SC} twice, SC 8, {2SC} twice, SC 8. 42

ROUND 47. SC 21, {2SC} twice, SC 8, {2SC} twice, SC 10. 46

ROUND 48. SC 21, {2SC} twice, 2SCtog, SC 8, 2SCtog, {2SC} twice, SC 10. 48

Upper Jaw

To create jaw you'll switch from working in rounds to working in rows, turning the piece after each row.

ROUND 1. Begin by Chaining 1 and turning piece, continuing from where you left off on Round 48; SC 37, Ch 1, turn. 37

ROUND 2. {2SCtog} twice, SC 29, {2SCtog} twice, Ch 1, turn. 33

ROUND 3. SC 6, 2SCtog, SC 17, 2SCtog, SC 6, Ch 1, turn. 31

ROUND 4. 3DC, SC 29, 3DC, Ch 1, turn. 35

ROUND 5. SC 1, 2SCtog, SC 29, 2SCtog, SC 1, Ch 1, turn. 33

ROUND 6. 2SCtog, SC 29, 2SCtog, Ch 1, turn. 31

ROUND 7. SC 6, 2SCtog, SC 15, 2SCtog, SC 6, Ch 1, turn. 29

ROUND 8. SC 5, {2SCtog} twice, SC 11, {2SCtog} twice, SC 5, Ch 1, turn. 25

ROUND 9. SC 3, {2SCtog, twice, SC 11, {2SCtog} twice, SC 5, Ch 1, turn. 21

ROUND 10. SC 3, 2SCtog, SC 11, 2SCtog, SC 3, Ch 1, turn. 19

ROUNDS 11-21. SC across, Ch 1, turn. 19

ROUND 22. 2SCtog, SC 15, 2SCtog, Ch 1, turn. 17

ROW 23. 2SCtog, SC 13, 2SCtog, Ch 1, turn. 15

ROUND 24. {2SCtog} twice, SC 9, {2SCtog} twice, Ch 1, turn. 13

ROUND 25. {2SCtog} twice, SC 5, {2SCtog} twice, Ch 1, turn. 9

ROUND 26. {2SCtog} twice, SC 1, {2SCtog} twice, Ch 1, turn. 5

Finish off.

Edging

JWSC at left side of upper jaw (when upside down) and SC around edge for a total of 54 stitches.

Bottom Jaw

FOUNDATION: With alligator upside down, JWSC to same stitch that you started the edging for Upper jaw.

ROUND 1. SC across, ending where the last stitch of edging does, Ch 1, turn. 13

ROUNDS 2-9. SC across, Ch 1, turn. 13

ROUND 10. SC 1, 2SCtog, SC 7, 2SCtog, SC 1, Ch 1, turn. 11

ROUND 11-20. SC across, Ch 1, turn. 11

ROUND 21. 2SCtog, SC 7, 2SCtog, Ch 1, turn. 9

Finish off.

Edging

FOUNDATION: JWSC at left side of upper jaw (when upside down) and SC around edge for a total of 48 stitches, Ch 1, turn. 48

EDGING ROW 1. 2SCtog, SC 42, 2SCtog, Ch 1, turn. 46

EDGING ROW 2. SS 3, SC 40, SS 3. Finish off.

Lower Insert

FOUNDATION: Begin with DMC #3328, Ch 13, turn. 13

ROUND 1. Beginning in second Ch from hook;

SC across, Ch 1, turn. 12

ROUNDS 2-9. SC across

ROUND 10. SC 5, 2SCtog, SC 5. 11

ROUNDS 11-17. SC across, Ch 1, turn. 11

ROUND 18. 2SCtog, SC 7, 2SCtog, Ch 1, turn. 9

ROUND 19. 2SCtog, SC 5, 2SCtog, Ch 1, turn. 7

Finish off

Edging

Join at right hand corner and SC all around edge. 39

Teeth

FOUNDATION: With DMC White, begin on left hand side; SC around posts of edge stitches beginning at post between 5th and 6th stitch from corner, for 28 stitches, Ch 1, turn. 28

ROUND 1. *SC 1, Ch 1, SS 1* across row. 14 teeth, 42 stitches

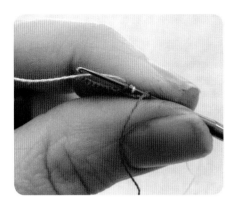

Upper Insert

FOUNDATION: Begin with DMC #3328, Ch 16, turn. 16

ROUND 1. Beginning in second Ch from hook, SC across, Ch 1, turn. 15

ROUNDS 2-19. SC across, Ch 1, turn. 15

ROUND 20. 2SCtog, SC 11, 2SCtog, Ch 1, turn. 13

ROUND 21. {2SCtog} twice, SC 5, {2SCtog} twice, Ch 1, turn. 9
Finish off.

Edging

Join at right hand corner and SC all around edge. 51

Teeth

FOUNDATION: With DMC White, begin on left hand side; SC around posts of edge stitches beginning at post between 6th and 7th stitch from corner, for 40 stitches, Ch 1, turn. 40

ROUND 1. *SC 1, Ch 1, SS 1* across row. 20 teeth, 60 stitches

Legs {Make 4}

FOUNDATION: Ch 2, SC 6 in second Ch from hook. 6

ROUND 1. *2SC in each* around. 12

ROUND 2. *SC 1, 2SC in next* around. 18

ROUND 3. *SC 2, 2SC in next* around. 24

ROUND 4. SC 10, {2SCtog} five times in back loop only , SC 4. 19

ROUND 5. SC 8, {2SCtog} four times, SC 3. 15

ROUND 6. SC 8, {2SCtog} twice, SC 3. 13

ROUNDS 7-12. SC around. 13

Finish off.

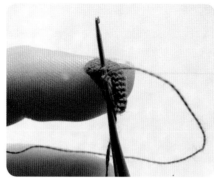

Working the Toes

JWSC to third stitch for Row 4, working in the front loop only; *SC 1, Ch 1, DC 1, Ch 1, SC 1* repeat four times and finish off.

Nostrils {Make 2}

FOUNDATION: Ch 2, 5DC in second Ch from hook. 5

Finish off

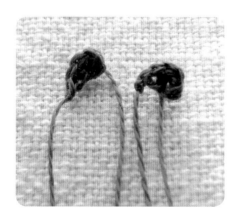

Assembly

STEP 1: Stuff body fully and let stuffing extend into upper jaw.

STEP 2: Sew upper jaw insert into upper jaw, going through only the top loops of the stitches so your thread won't how through either side.

STEP 3: Sew lower jaw and upper jaw together at ends.

STEP 4: Sew lower jaw insert into lower jaw using the same method as for upper jaw.

STEP 5: Using a long thread, loop through the head where you made the extra stitches. This will give a recessed area to sew on your eyes.

STEP 6: Sew eyes into recesses you just made. For this project I recommend going with beads or small buttons, something a little larger and shinier than a French knot looks best

STEP 7: Sew nostrils to front of upper jaw.

STEP 8: Take legs and pinch them sideways, then sew to body at evenly spaced intervals.

STEP 9: JWSS to back of body just above the tail, work a chain back and forth across the back of body in a zigzag pattern.

1

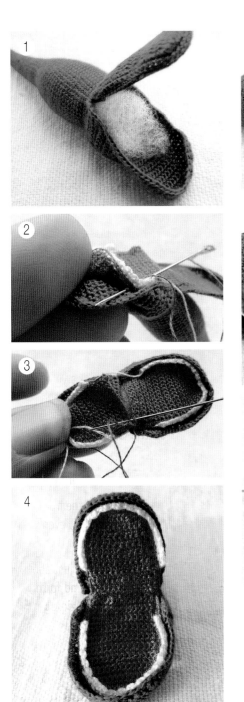

2

3

4

5

6

7

8

9

Buzzing Bees and a Hive

Abbreviations

SC: Single Crochet

2SC: Single Crochet twice in same stitch

2SCTOG: Single Crochet two stitches together, or decrease

3DC: Double Crochet three times into same stitch

SS: Slip Stitch

**: Repeat indicated directions across row

{}: Directions in brackets will be repeated a specified number of times

Materials

1+ Skeins of DMC #725 for hive, work with two strands.

Less than 1 skein of DMC #3078 for bees.

Less than 1 skein of DMC #535 for bees.

Less than 1 skein of DMC White for wings.

Size 10 crochet hook for double strand.

Size 12 crochet hook for single strand.

Small to medium black beads for eyes.

Sewing needle.

Hive

Top

FOUNDATION: DMC #725; Ch 2, SC 7 in second Ch from hook. 7

ROUND 1. *2SC in each* around. 14

ROUND 2. *SC 1, 2SC in next* around. 21

ROUND 3. *SC 2, 2SC in next* around. 28

ROUND 4. *SC 3, 2SC in next* around. 35

ROUNDS 5-7. SC around. 35

ROUND 8. *SC 3, 2SCtog* around. 28

ROUND 9. In front loop only, *SC 1, 2SC in next* around. 42

ROUND 10. SC around. 42

ROUND 11. *SC 2, 2SC in next* around. 56

ROUNDS 12-13. SC around. 56

ROUND 14. *SC 2, 2SCtog* around. 42

ROUND 15. In front loop only, *SC 2, 2SC in next* around. 56

ROUND 16. *SC 3, 2SC in next* around. 70

ROUNDS 17-19. SC around. 70

ROUND 20. *SC 3, 2SCtog* around. 56

ROUNDS 21-25. SC around. 56

Finish off

Bottom

FOUNDATION: DMC#725; Ch 2, SC 7 in second Ch from hook. 7

ROUND 1. *2SC in each* around. 14

ROUND 2. *SC 1, 2SC in next* around. 21

ROUND 3. *SC 2, 2SC in next* around. 28

ROUND 4. *SC 3, 2SC in next* around. 35

ROUND 5. SC around. 35

ROUND 6. *SC 4, 2SC in next* around. 42

ROUND 7. *SC 5, 2SC in next* around. 49

ROUND 8. SC around. 49

ROUND 9. *SC 6, 2SC in next* around. 56

ROUND 10. *SC 7, 2SC in next* around. 63

ROUND 11. SC in back loop only, around. 63

ROUNDS 12-16. SC around. 63

Finish off

Queen Bee

FOUNDATION: Begin with DMC #3078; Ch 2, SC 6 in second Ch from hook. 6

ROUND 1. *2SC in each* around. 12

ROUND 2. *SC 1, 2SC in next* around. 18

ROUND 3. *SC 2, 2SC in next* around. 24

ROUND 4. *SC 3, 2SC in next* around. 30

ROUNDS 5-8. SC around. 30

ROUND 9. *SC 3, 2SCtog* around. 24

ROUND 10. *2SCtog * around. 12

ROUND 11. Switch to DMC #535; *2SC in each* around. 24

ROUND 12. SC around. 24

ROUNDS 13-14. Switch back to DMC #3078; SC around. 24

ROUND 15. Switch back to DMC #535; {2SC} five times, SC 19.

ROUND 16. {SC 1, 2SC in next} five times, SC 19. 24

ROUND 17. Switch back to DMC #3078; SC around. 24

ROUND 18. {SC 1, 2SCtog} five times, SC 19. 24

ROUND 19. *2SCtog* around. 12

Stuff firmly, finish off in your preferred method

Queen Bee Parts

Stinger

FOUNDATION: With DMC #535; Ch 2, SC 6 in second Ch from hook. 6

ROUND 1. SC in back loop only. 6

ROUND 2. 2SCtog, SC 4. 5

ROUND 3. 2SCtog, SC 3. 4

ROUND 4. {2SCtog} twice. 2

Wings

FOUNDATION: With DMC White; {Ch 9, 3DC in 6th Ch from hook, Ch 3, SS into first Ch} four times, finish off.

Antennae

FOUNDATION: With DMC #535; Ch 9, SC in second Ch from hook, {2HDC} twice, SS in next 5, finish off.

Worker Bees

Body

FOUNDATION: With DMC #3078; Ch 2, SC 6 in second Ch from hook. 6

ROUND 1. *2SC in each* around. 12

ROUND 2. *SC 1, 2SC in next* around. 18

ROUNDS 3-5. SC around. 18

ROUND 6. *2SCtog* around. 9

ROUND 7. Switch to DMC #535; SC around. 9

ROUND 8. *2SC in each* around. 18

ROUNDS 9-10. Switch to DMC #3078; SC around. 18

ROUNDS 11-12. Switch to DMC #535; *2SCtog* around. 9

Wings

FOUNDATION: With DMC White; {Ch 5, 2SC in second Ch from hook, Ch 4, SS into first Ch} four times, finish off.

Antennae

FOUNDATION: With DMC# 535; Ch 6, SC in second Ch from hook, {HDC, SC} in next stitch, SS in next 3, finish off.

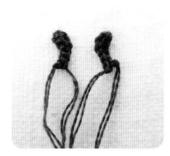

Assembly

Queen bee

STEP 1: Sew wings to upper middle back.

STEP 2: Sew stinger to bottom on the extend portion created on between rows 15-18.

STEP 3: Sew antennae to upper head, keeping in line with each other.

STEP 4: Add French knots or small beads for eyes.

STEP 5: Embroider eyebrows.

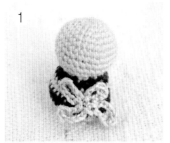

Worker bees

STEP 1: Sew wings to upper middle back

STEP 2: Sew antennae to upper head, keeping in line with each other.

STEP 3: Add French knots or small beads for eyes

STEP 4: Embroider eye brows.

If desired you can sew one or more worker bees to hive, or just leave them loose.

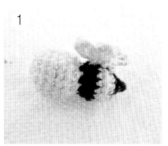
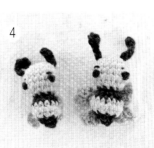

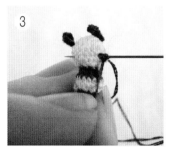

Humpfrey

Abbreviations

SC: Single Crochet

2SC: Single Crochet twice in same stitch

2SCTOG: Single Crochet two stitches together, or decrease

3SCTOG: Single crochet three stitches together.

SS: Slip Stitch

**: Repeat indicated directions across row

{}: Directions in brackets will be repeated a specified number of times

Materials

2 Skeins of DMC #3829 for all of body,
Less than a skein of DMC #780 for nose and detail embroidery
Size 10 crochet hook for double strand
Size 12 crochet hook for single strand
Small black beads for eyes (Optional)
Sewing needle

Head

FOUNDATION: With DMC #3829; Ch 2, SC 6 in second Ch from hook. 6

ROUND 1. *2SC in each* around. 12

ROUND 2. *SC 1, 2SC in next* around. 18

ROUND 3. *SC 2, 2SC in next* around. 24

ROUND 4. {SC 3, 2SC} five times, SC 1, 3SCtog. 27

ROUND 5. 2SC, SC 3, 2SC, {SC 4, 2SC} five times, 2SC, SS. 36

ROUND 6. {2SC} twice, SC 10, 2SC, SC 5, 2SC, SC 11, 2SC, SC 1,
2SC, SS. 42

ROUND 7. {SC 1, 2SC} twice, SC 29, {SC 2,

2SC} twice, SS. 44

ROUND 8. SC 16, 2SCtog, SC 5, 2SCtog, SC 18, SS. 42

ROUND 9. SC 9, 2SCtog, {SC 4, 2SCtog} three times, SC 12, SS. 38

ROUND 10. SC 35, 2SCtog, SS. 37

ROUND 11. {2SCtog} three times , SC 23, {2SCtog} three times . 31

ROUND 12. SC 30, skip SS. 30

ROUNDS 13–15. 2SCtog, SC 8, 2SC, SC 4, 2SC, SC 11, 2SCtog. 30

ROUNDS 16-21. SC around . 30

ROUND 22. SC 10, {SC 1, 2SC} five times, SC 10. 35

ROUND 23. 2SC, SC 1, 2SC, SC 8, 2SCtog, SC 1, 2SCtog SC 3, 2SCtog, SC 1, 2SCtog, SC 8, 2SC, SC 1, 2SC. 35

ROUNDS 24-26. SC around. 35

ROUND 27. SC 10, 2SCtog, {SC 3, 2SCtog] four times, SC 8. 30

ROUND 28. SC 9, 2SCtog, {SC 2, 2SCtog} four times, SC 8. 25

ROUNDS 29-34. 2SC, SC 10, {2SCtog} twice, SC 11, 2SC. 25

ROUNDS 34-36. SC around. 25

Finish off and stuff firm, keeping the final shape in mind.

Bactrian Hump {Make 2}

FOUNDATION: With DMC #3829; Ch 2, SC 5 in second Ch from hook. 5

ROUND 1. *2SC in each* around. 10

ROUND 2. *SC 1, 2SC in next* around. 15

ROUND 3. *SC 2, 2SC in next* around. 20

ROUND 4. *SC 3, 2SC in next* around. 25

ROUND 5. *SC 4, 2SC in next* around. 30

ROUND 6. SC around. 30

ROUND 7. *SC 5, 2SC in next* around. 35

ROUND 8. SC around. 35

ROUND 9. *SC 6, 2SC in next* around. 40

ROUND 10. SC around. 40

Finish off.

Joining Bactrian Humps to form body

Align Bactrian humps side by side and whip stitch or SC together over 10 stitches.

ROUND 1-11. SC around. 60

ROUND 12. *SC 8 , 2SCtog* around. 54

ROUND 13. *SC 7, 2SCtog* around. 48

ROUND 14. *SC 6, 2SCtog* around. 42

ROUND 15. *SC 5, 2SCtog* around. 36

ROUND 16. *SC 4, 2SCtog* around. 30

ROUND 17. *SC 3, 2SCtog* around. 24

ROUND 18. *SC 2, 2SCtog* around. 18

ROUND 19. *2SCtog* around. 9

Stuff firmly, finish with your preferred method.

Ears {Make 2}

FOUNDATION: With DMC #3829; Ch 6, turn. 6

ROUND 1. Beginning in second Ch from hook, SC across. 5

ROUND 2-3. SC, Ch 1, turn. 5

ROUND 4. 2SCtog, SC 1, 2SCtog. 3

Finish off.

Tail

FOUNDATION: Ch 9.

Finish off, leaving long tails both at the beginning and end of piece

Dromedary Hump

FOUNDATION: Ch 2, SC 6 in second Ch from hook. 6
ROUND 1. *2SC in each* around. 12
ROUND 2. *SC 1, 2SC in next* around. 18
ROUND 3. *SC 2, 2SC in next* around. 24
ROUND 4. *SC 3, 2SC in next* around. 30
ROUND 5. SC around. 30
ROUND 6. *SC 4, 2SC in next* around. 36
ROUND 7. SC around. 36
ROUND 8. *SC 5, 2SC in next* around. 42
ROUND 9. *SC 6, 2SC in next* around. 48
ROUND 10. SC around. 48
ROUND 11. *SC 7, 2SC in next* around. 54
ROUNDS 12-18. SC around. 54
ROUNDS 19. *SC 7, 2SCtog* around. 48
ROUND 20. SC 2, 2SCtog* around. 36
ROUND 21. *SC 1, 2SCtog* around. 24
ROUND 22. *2SCtog* around. 12
ROUND 23. SC around. 12
ROUND 24. *2SCtog* around. 6
Stuff Firm, finish with your preferred method.

Legs {Make 4}

FOUNDATION: Ch 2, SC 6 in second Ch from hook. 6
ROUND 1. *2SC in each* around. 12
ROUND 2. *SC 1, 2SC in next* across. 18
ROUND 3. *SC in back loop only* around. 18
ROUNDS 4-6. SC around. 18
ROUND 7. 2SCtog, SC 16. 17
ROUND 8. 2SCtog, SC 15. 16
ROUND 9. 2SCtog, SC 14. 15
ROUND 10. 2SCtog, SC 13. 14
ROUND 11. 2SCtog, SC 12. 13
ROUND 12. 2SCtog, SC 11. 12
ROUNDS 13-15. SC around. 12
ROUND 16. SC 10, {2SC} twice. 14
ROUND 17. SC 10, {SC 1, 2SC} twice. 16
ROUND 18. SC 10, {SC 1, 2SCtog} twice. 14
ROUND 19. SC 10, {2SCtog} twice. 12
ROUNDS 20-23. SC around. 12
ROUND 24. *2SCtog* around. 6
Stuff firmly up to the knee and finish in your preferred method.

Toes {Make 8}

FOUNDATION: Ch 2, SC 6 in second Ch from hook. 6
ROUND 1. *2SC in each* across. 12
ROUNDS 2-4. SC around. 12
ROUND 5. *SC 1, 2SCtog* around. 8
SC 6-7. SC around. 8

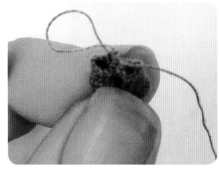

Join two toes together by Single Crocheting around one toe and then the other without finishing off in between. 16
ROUNDS 1-4. SC around. 16
ROUND 5. *2SCtog* around. 8
Stuff only the toes firmly, finish in your preferred method.

Assembly

STEP 1: Sew finished toes to bottom of legs (which is the part worked first).

STEP 2: Sew head to lower middle on body, on a narrow end so the humps lines up with the head.

STEP 3: Sew legs onto under side of body, place them a bit toward the middle

STEP 4: Take chain made for tail and fold in half, use long tails to secure to backside of camel hump.

STEP 5: Sew ears to upper sides of head (at the bend)

STEP 6: Add French knots or small beads for eyes.

STEP 7 : Embroider a nose and eyebrows with DMC #780

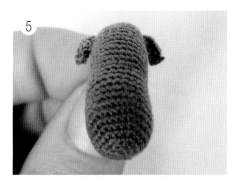

camellia

Abbreviations

SC: Single Crochet
2SC: Single Crochet twice in same stitch
2SCTOG: Single Crochet two stitches together, or decrease
HDC: Half Double Crochet
SS: Slip Stitch
**: Repeat indicated directions across row
{}: Directions in brackets will be repeated a specified number of times

Materials

Skeins of DMC #3819 for all of body.
Less than a skein of DMC #907 for detail embroidery
Size 10 crochet hook for double strand.
Size 12 crochet hook for single strand.
Small to medium black beads for eyes (optional).
Sewing needle

Head and Body

FOUNDATION: With DMC #3819; Ch 2, SC 6 in second Ch from hook. 6
ROUND 1. *2SC in each* around. 12
ROUND 2. SC 4, {SC 1, 2SC} four times. 16
ROUND 3. SC 4, {SC 2, 2SC} four times. 20
ROUND 4. SC 4, {SC 3, 2SC} four times. 24
ROUND 5. SC 4, {SC 4, 2SC} four times. 28
ROUND 6. SC around. 28
ROUND 7. SC 4, {SC 5, 2SC} four times. 32
ROUND 8. SC 4, {SC 6, 2SC} four times. 36
ROUND 9. SC 13, {2SC} twice, SC 15, {2SC} twice, SC . 40
ROUND 10. SC 13, {SC 1, 2SC} twice, SC 15, {SC 1, 2SC} twice, SC 4. 44
ROUND 11. SC 13, {SC 2, SC 1} three times, SC 15, {2SC, SC 1} three times, SC 4. 50
ROUND 12. SC around. 50
ROUND 13. SC 13, {2SCtog, SC 1} three times, SC 15, {2SCtog, SC 1} three times, SC 4. 44
ROUNDS 14-15. SC around. 44
ROUND 16. SC 13, {SC 1, 2SCtog} twice, SC 15, {SC 1, 2SCtog} twice, SC 4. 40
ROUNDS 17-19. SC around. 40

ROUND 20. *SC 2, 2SCtog* around. 30
ROUND 21. *SC 1, 2SCtog* around. 20
ROUND 22. *2SCtog* around. 10
ROUND 23. *2SC in each* around. 20
ROUND 24. *SC 1, 2SC in next* around. 30
Stuff head firmly here.
ROUNDS 25-26. SC around. 30
ROUND 28. SC 18, {2SC} twice, SC 10. 32
ROUND 29. SC 18, {SC 1, 2SC} twice, SC 10. 34
ROUNDS 30-34. SC around. 34
ROUND 35. SC 18, {SC 1, 2SCtog} twice, SC 10. 32
ROUNDS 36-37. SC around. 32
ROUND 38. SC 18, {2SCtog} twice, SC 10. 30
ROUND 39. *SC 1, 2SCtog* around. 20
ROUNDS 40-41. SC around. 20
ROUNDS 42-44. SC 3, 2SC, SC 8, 2SCtog, SC 6. 20
Stuff body firmly here.
ROUND 45. SC 12, 2SCtog, SC 6. 19
ROUNDS 46-48. SC 3, 2SC, SC 7, 2SCtog, SC 6. 19
ROUND 49. SC 11, 2SCtog, SC 6. 18
ROUNDS 50-52. SC 3 2SC, SC 6, 2SCtog, SC 6. 18

ROUND 53. SC 10, 2SCtog, SC 6. 17
ROUNDS 54-56. SC 3, 2SC, SC 5, 2SCtog, SC 6. 17
ROUND 57. SC 9, 2SCtog, SC 6. 16
ROUNDS 58-59. SC 3, 2SC, SC 4, 2SCtog, SC 6. 16
ROUND 60. SC 8, 2SCtog, SC 6. 15
ROUND 61-64. SC 3, 2SC, SC 3, 2SCtog, SC 6. 15
ROUND 65. SC 7, 2SCtog, SC 6. 14
ROUND 66-67. SC 3, 2SC, SC 2, 2SCtog, SC 6. 14
ROUND 68. SC 6, 2SCtog, SC 6. 13
ROUNDS 69-70. SC 3, 2SC, SC 1, 2SCtog, SC 6. 13
ROUND 71. SC 5, 2SCtog, SC 6. 12
ROWS 72-78. SC 3, 2SC, 2SCtog, SC 6. 12
ROUND 79. SC 4, 2SCtog, SC 6. 11
ROUND 80. SC 9, 2SCtog. 10
ROUND 81. SC around. 10

You'll need to stuff the tail as you go, partly to help shape the curve, and partly because you won't be able to stuff it as you progress
ROUND 82. SC 8, 2SCtog. 9
ROUNDS 83-85. SC around. 9
ROUNDS 86. SC 7, 2SCtog. 8
ROUNDS 87-89. SC around. 8
ROUND 90. SC 6, 2SCtog. 7
ROUNDS 91-93. SC around. 7
ROUND 94. SC 5, 2SCtog. 6
ROUNDS 95-96. SC around. 6
ROUND 97. SC 4, 2SCtog. 5
ROUNDS 98-99. SC around. 5
ROUND 100. SC 3, 2SCtog. 4
ROUNDS 101-103. SC around. 4
ROUND 104. SC 2, 2SCtog. 3
ROUNDS 105-107. SC around. 3
ROUND 108. 3SCtog. 1
Finish off and weave in yarn end.

Toes {Make 8}

FOUNDATION: DMC #3819; Ch 2, SC 6 in second Ch from hook. 6
ROUNDS 1-4. SC around. 6
Finish off.

Eyes {Make 2}

Outer Eye

FOUNDATION: With DMC #3819; Ch 2, SC 6 in second Ch from hook. 6
ROUND 1. SC in back loop only, around. 6
ROUNDS 2-4. SC around. 6
Finish off

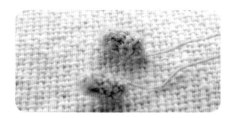

To Join Toes

Join two toes with two stitches each. You can use single crochet or whip stitch them. This will give you 8 stitches when you crochet around the toes.

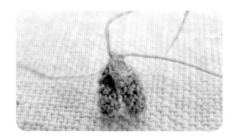

Comb {Optional}

FOUNDATION: With DMC #3819 Ch 12, turn
ROWS 1-2. SC across Round, Ch 1, turn. 11
ROUND 3. 2SCtog, SC 9, Ch 1, turn. 10
ROUND 4. SC 8, 2SCtog, Ch 1, turn. 9
ROUND 5. 2SCtog, SC 7, Ch 1, turn. 8
ROUND 6. SC 6, 2SCtog, Ch 1, turn. 7
ROUND 7. 2SCtog, SC 3, 2SCtog, Ch 1, turn. 5
ROUND 8. SC 12 along outside edge. 12
Finish off

Legs {Make 4}

With a finished pair of toes and still using DMC #3819
ROUND 1. SC around outside of toes, picking up an extra on each side. 10
ROUND 2. SC around. 10
ROUND 3. *2SCtog* around. 5
ROUNDS 4-10. SC around. 5
Finish off, do not stuff.

Eyestalk

FOUNDATION: Ch 2, SC 5 in second Ch from hook. 5
ROUNDS 1-3. SC around. 5
Finish off, attach medium sized black bead to end of stalk

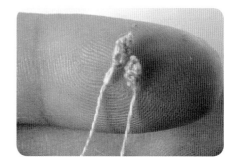

Assembly

STEP 1: With body colored thread, run a loop through the head where you made the extra stitches on rounds 9-16. Pull thread tight to make indents for the eyes.

STEP 2: Sew eyestalk and outer eye together.

STEP 3: Use French knots or small beads to make pupils.

STEP 4: Sew finished eyes to head in the indents made in step 1.

STEP 5: Sew a pair of legs to either side of upper body.

STEP 6: Sew the final pair of legs in line with the first to either side of lower body.

STEP 7: Curl tail into a spiral and sew in place.

STEP 8: If desired, sew comb to middle of head.

STEP 9: Embroider mouth and other small details.

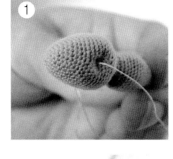

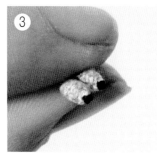

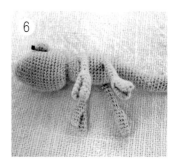
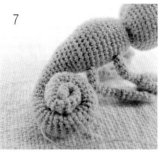

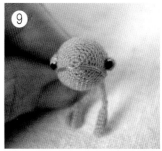

Pinkerton

Abbreviations

SC: Single Crochet

2SC: Single Crochet twice in same stitch

2SCTOG: Single Crochet two stitches together, or decrease

3DC: Double Crochet three times in the same stitch

2HDC: Half Double Crochet twice in same stitch

HDC: Half Double Crochet

JWSC: Join with Single Crochet

SS: Slip Stitch

**: Repeat indicated directions across row

{}: Directions in brackets will be repeated a specified number of times

Materials

1 Skein of DMC #3706 for of body.

Less than 1 skein of DMC #963 for wings.

Less than 1 skein of DMC #3708 for wing tips.**

Less than 1 skein of DMC #415 for beginning of beak.

Less than 1 skein of DMC #414 for remainder of beak.

Less than 1 skein of DMC #822 for legs.

Size 10 crochet hook for double stand

Size 12 crochet hook for single strand.

Small to medium black beads for eyes.**

Sewing needle

Body

FOUNDATION: With DMC #3706; Ch 2, SC 7 in second Ch from hook. 7

ROUND 1. {2SC} three times, {2HDC} four times. 14

ROUND 2. {SC 1, 2SC} three times, {HDC 1, 2HDC} four times. 21

ROUND 3. {SC 2, 2SC} three times, {HDC 2, 2HDC} four times. 28

ROUND 4. {SC 3, 2SC} three times, {HDC 3, 2HDC} four times. 35

ROUND 5. SC 15, {SC 4, 2SC} four times. 39

ROUND 6. SC 15, {SC 5, 2SC} four times. 43

ROUND 7. SC 15, {SC 6, 2SC} four times. 47

ROUND 8. SC 23, {SC 7, 2SC} twice, SC 8. 49

ROUND 9. SC 23, {SC 8, 2SC} twice, SC 8. 51

ROUND 10. SC 36, {2SC} twice, SC 13. 53

ROUND 11. SC 37, {2SC} twice, SC 14. 55

ROUND 12. SC 38, {2SC} twice, SC 15. 57

ROUND 13. {SC 3, 2SCtog} three times, SC 42. 54

ROUND 14. SC 3, Ch 6, skip 9, SC 36. 54

ROUND 15. SC around. 54

ROUND 16. *SC 4, 2SCtog* around. 45

ROUND 17. *SC 3, 2SCtog* around. 36

ROUND 18. *SC 2, 2SCtog* around. 27

ROUND 19. *SC 1, 2SCtog* around. 18

ROUND 20. *2SCtog* around. 9

Stuff firmly, finish off in your preferred method.

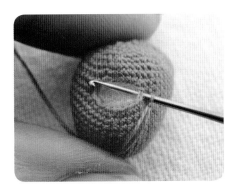

Neck and Head

FOUNDATION: With DMC #3706; JWSC to bottom right corner or body opening.

ROUND 1. SC around opening for a total of 20 stitches. 20

ROUNDS 2-19. SC around. 21

If you have not already done so, stuff body firmly after Round 3 or 4. Stuff the neck gradually as you go, curving it along the way.

ROUND 20. SC 2, 2SCtog, SC 17. 20

ROUND 21. SC 1, {2SCtog} four times, SC 7. 16

ROUNDS 22-28. SC 2, 2SCtog, SC 6, 2SC, SC 5. 16

ROUND 29. *SC 3, 2SC in next* around. 20

ROUND 30. *SC 4, 2SC in next* around. 24

ROUND 31. *SC 5, 2SC in next* around. 28

ROUND 32. *SC 6, 2SC in next* around. 32

ROUNDS 33-38. SC around. 32

ROUND 39. *SC 6, 2SCtog* around. 28

ROUND 40. *SC 5, 2SCtog* around. 24

ROUND 41. *SC 4, 2SCtog* around. 20

Here you will switch colors and begin working the beak.

Beak

Foundation: Begin where Round 41 leaves off with DMC #415;

ROUNDS 42-44. SC around. 20

ROUNDS 44-46. Switch to DMC #414;

ROUND 47. SC 14, {SC 1, 2SC} three times. 23

ROUNDS 48-49. SC around. 23

ROUND 50. SC 14, {SC 1, 2SCtog} three times. 20

ROUND 51. SC 6, {2SC} twice, SC 12. 22

ROUND 52. SC 7, {2SC} twice, SC 7, {2SCtog} three times. 21

ROUND 53. SC around. 21

ROUND 54. SC 17, {2SCtog} twice. 19

ROUND 55. SC 2, 2SCtog, SC 4, 2SC, SC 4, 2SCtog, SC 2. 17

ROUND 56. {2SCtog} twice, SC 9, {2SCtog} twice. 13

ROUND 57. {2SCtog} twice, SC 5, {2SCtog} twice. 9

Stuff head and beak firm and finish with ladder stitch.

Legs {Make 2}

FOUNDATION: Begin with DMC #822; Ch 2, SC 6 in second Ch from hook. 6

ROUNDS 1- 21. SC around. 6

ROUND 22. {3DC} three times, {2SC} three times. 15

ROUND 23. SC 1, {DC, Ch 1, DC} in same stitch, SC 1* three times.

Finish off, insert wire into legs to hold upright.

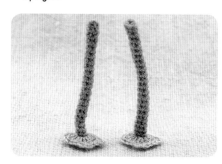

Upper Leg Piece {Make 2}

FOUNDATION: Begin with DMC #3706; Ch 2, SC 6 in second Ch from hook. 6

ROUND 1. *2SC* around. 12

ROUND 2. SC in back loop only. 12

ROUNDS 3-4. SC around. 12

ROUND 5. *2SCtog* around. 6

Finish off

Wings {Make 2}

FOUNDATION: Begin with DMC #963; Ch 12, turn. 12

ROUND 1. Begin in second Ch from hook, SC 10, 3SC in last stitch, SC 10 in back loop of foundation. CH 3 turn. 26

ROUND 2. SC 13, 3SC, SC 8, Ch 3 turn. 27

ROUND 3. SC 11, 3SC, SC 13, Ch 1, turn. 27

ROUND 4. SC 14, 3SC, SC 11, Ch 1, turn. 28

ROUND 5. SC 12, 3SC, SC 12, Ch 2, turn. 29

ROUND 6. SC 14, 3SC. 17

**Optional, Use 3708 to SC along back edge of wing for more contrast.

Finish off

Assembly

STEP 1: Sew wings to either side of body at an angle towards the point of back.

STEP 2: Insert wire into leg.

STEP 3: Insert leg into outer leg, secure in place with small stitches.

STEP 4: Sew finished legs to underside of body.

STEP 5: Add French knots or small beads for eyes, just above and out side of beak.

STEP 6: Embroider eyebrows.

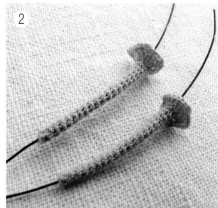

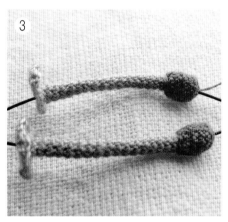

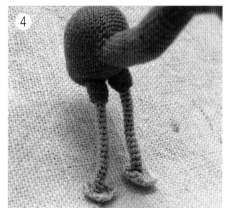

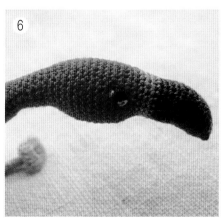

ollie otter

Abbreviations

SC: Single Crochet
2SC: Single Crochet twice in same stitch
2SCTOG: Single Crochet two stitches together, or decrease
SS: Slip Stitch
**: Repeat indicated directions across row
{}: Directions in brackets will be repeated a specified number of times
Numbers at the end of rows indicate number of stitches in that row.

Materials

1+ skeins of DMC #3023 for body, arms and legs.
Less than a skein of DMC #840 for Tips of arms, feet, tail, and detail embroidery.
Size 10 crochet hook for double strand.
Size 12 hook for single strand.
Small black beads for eyes (Optional).
Sewing needle.

Body

FOUNDATION: Begin with DMC #3023 Ch 2, SC 6 in second Ch from hook. 6
ROUND 1. *2SC in each* around. 12
ROUND 2. *SC 1, 2SC in next* around. 18
ROUND 3. *SC 2, 2SC in next* around. 24
ROUND 4. *SC 3, 2SC in next* around. 30
ROUND 5. *SC 4, 2SC in next* around. 36
ROUND 6. *SC 5, 2SC in next* around. 42
ROUND 7. *SC 6, 2SC in next* around. 48
ROUNDS 8-11. SC around. 48
ROUND 12. *SC 14, 2SC around. 51
ROUND 13-14. SC around. 51
ROUND 15. *SC 14, 2SCtog in next* around. 48
ROUND 16. SC around. 48
ROUND 17. *SC 6, 2SCtog* around. 42
ROUND 18. *SC 5, 2SCtog* around. 36
ROUND 19. *2SCtog* around. 18
ROUNDS 20-22. SC around. 18
Stuff head here, firmly.
ROUND 23. *SC 8, 2SC in next* around. 20
ROUND 24. *SC 9, 2SC in next* around. 22
ROUND 25. *SC 10, 2SC in next* around. 24
ROUND 26. *SC 11, 2SC in next* around. 26
ROUND 27. *SC 12, 2SC in next* around. 28
ROUND 28. *SC 13, 2SC in next* around. 30
ROUND 29. *SC 14, 2SC in next* around. 32
ROUND 30. *SC 15, 2SC in next* around. 34

ROUND 31. *SC 16, 2SC in next* around. 36
Head, after stuffing.
ROUNDS 32-37. SC around. 36
ROUND 38. SC 17, {SC 2, 2SC in next} five times, SC 2. 41
ROUND 39. SC 17, {SC 3, 2SC in next} five times, SC 2. 46
ROUNDS 40-42. SC around. 46
ROUND 43. SC 17, {SC 3, 2SCtog} five times, SC 2. 41
ROUND 44. SC 17, {SC 2, 2SCtog} five times, SC 2. 36

ROUND 45. SC 17, 2SCtog, SC 14, 2SCtog. 34

ROUND 46. {2SCtog} nine times, SC 15. 25

ROUND 47. SC around. 25

ROUND 48. *SC 3, 2SCtog* around. 20

ROUNDS 49-51. SC around. 20

ROUND 52. *SC 8, 2SCtog* around. 18

ROUNDS 53-57. SC around. 18

ROUND 58. *SC 7, 2SCtog* around. 16

ROUNDS 59-60. SC around. 16

ROUND 61. Switch to DMC #840, *SC 6, 2SCtog* around. 14

ROUNDS 62-63. SC around. 14

ROUND 64. *SC 5, 2SCtog* around. 12

ROUND 65. *SC 4, 2SCtog* around. 10

ROUND 66. *SC 3, 2SCtog* around. 8

Finish in your preferred method.
Body, after stuffing.

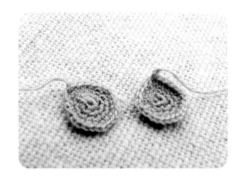

Shell {Make 2}

FOUNDATION: Begin with DMC #822, Ch 2, SC 8 in second Ch from hook. 8

ROUND 1. {2SC} five times, SC 3. 13

ROUND 2. SC 2, {SC 1, 2SC} three times, SC 5. 16

ROUND 3. SC 2, {SC 2, 2SC} three times, SC 5 19

Finish off.

To join shell halves, turn them both wrong side out and join together after last 2SC on each shell. Join with a SC and work 8 more along seam.

Pink Insert

FOUNDATION: Begin with DMC #225, Ch 2, SC 6 in second Ch from hook.

ROUND 1. {2SC} four times, SC 2. 10

Finish off.

Arms {Make 2}

FOUNDATION: Begin with DMC #840, Ch 2, SC 6 in second Ch from hook. 6
ROUND 1. *2SC in each* around. 12
ROUNDS 2-3. SC around. 12
ROUNDS 4-8. Switch to DMC# 3023, SC around.
12 ROUND 9. *SC 2, 2SCtog* around. 9
Finish off, stuff medium firm only in top of arms.

Ears {Make 2}

FOUNDATION: With DMC #3023 Ch 2, SC 7 in second Ch from hook. 7
ROUND 1. {2SC} three times, SC 4. 10
ROUND 2. SC around. 10
Finish off, fold flat with 2SC stitches at the back to create a bowl shape.

Snout

FOUNDATION: Begin with DMC #3023 Ch 2, SC 8, in second Ch from hook. 8
ROUND 1. SC 3, 2SC, SC 3, 2SC. 10
ROUND 2. SC 3, {2SC} twice, SC 3, {2SC} twice. 14
ROUND 3. SC 4, {2SC} twice, SC 5, {2SC} twice, SC 1. 18
ROUND 4. SC 5, {2SC} twice, SC 7, {2SC} twice, SC 2. 22
ROUND 5. SC 6, {2SC} twice, SC 9, {2SC} twice, SC 3. 26
Finish off.

Legs {Make 2}

FOUNDATION: Begin with DMC #840, Ch 2, SC 7 in second Ch from hook. 7
ROUND 1. *2SC in each* around. 14
ROUND 2. *SC 1, 2SC in next* around. 21
ROUND 3. {SC 2, 2SC} three times, SC 12 in back loop only. 24
ROUND 4. {SC 2, 2SCtog} three times, SC 12. 21
ROUND 5. {SC 1, 2SCtog} three times, SC 12. 18
ROUND 6. {2SCtog} three times, switch to DMC# 3023 , SC 12. 15
ROUNDS 7-9. SC around. 15
Finish off, stuff medium firm.

Assembly

STEP 1: Sew snout to lower center of face, stuff gently.

STEP 2: Fold ears and sew ears to lower sides of face.

STEP 3: Sew arms to upper sides of body.

STEP 4: Sew legs to lower side of body, keeping in line with the arms.

STEP 5: Sew shell to hands.

STEP 6: Use French knots or small beads to make eyes.

STEP 7: Embroider on some eyebrows.

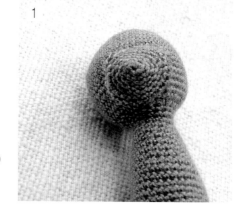

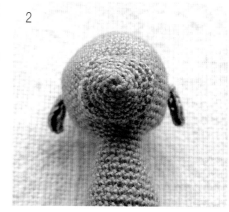

Narwhal

Abbreviations

SC: Single Crochet

2SC: Single Crochet twice in same stitch

2SCTOG: Single Crochet two stitches together, or decrease

HDC: Half Double Crochet

3DC: Double Crochet three in same space

SS: Slip Stitch

**: Repeat indicated directions across row

{}: Directions in brackets will be repeated a specified number of times

Materials

1 Skein of DMC #3072 for all of body.

Less than one skein DMC Ecru or White for horn.

Less than a skein of DMC #606 for heart

Size 10 crochet hook for double strand.

Size 12 crochet hook for single strand.

Small to medium black beads for eyes (optional).

Sewing needle

Body

FOUNDATION: With DMC #3072; Ch 2, SC 6 in second Ch from hook. 6

ROUND 1. *2SC in each* around. 12

ROUND 2. *SC 1, 2SC in next* around. 18

ROUND 3. *SC 2, 2SC in next* around. 24

ROUND 4. *SC 3, 2SC in next* around. 30

ROUND 5. *SC 4, 2SC in next* around. 36

ROUND 6. *SC 5, 2SC in next* around. 42

ROUNDS 7-12. SC around. 42

ROUND 13. *SC 5, 2SCtog* around. 36

ROUNDS 14-16. SC around

ROUND 17. *SC 4, 2SCtog* around. 30

ROUND 18. SC around. 30

ROUND 19. *SC 3, 2SCtog* around. 24

ROUNDS 20-23. SC around. 24

ROUND 24. {2SCtog} twice, SC 20. 22

ROUND 25. {2SCtog} twice, SC 18. 20

ROUND 26. {2SCtog} twice, SC 16. 18

ROUND 27. {2SCtog} twice, SC 14. 16

Stuff body here.

ROUND 28. Skip 8 stitches SC in 9th ** This becomes the first stitch of the tail fin.

Tail and Fins

Work first tail fin where Round 28 leaves off, still using DMC #3072.

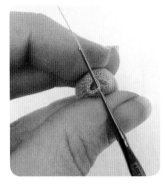

Begin second fin in 9th stitch of row 28.

ROUNDS 1-2. SC around. 8
ROUND 3. SC 3, {2SC} twice, SC 3. 10
ROUND 4. SC 4, {2SC} twice, SC 4. 12
ROUND 5. {2SCtog} twice, SC 4, {2SCtog} twice. 10

ROUND 6. *2SCtog* around. 5 Finish off, do not stuff tail.

Fins {Make 2}

FOUNDATION: With DMC #3072; Ch 2, SC 4 in second Ch from hook. 4
ROUND 1. {2SC} twice, SC 2. 6
ROUND 2. SC 1, {2SC} twice, SC 3. 8
ROUNDS 3-5. SC around. 8
ROUND 6. SC 2, 2SCtog, SC 4. 7
ROUND 7. SC around. Finish off, fold flat.

Heart

FOUNDATION: With DMC #606; Ch 4, 3DC in first Ch made, SC 1, Ch 2, SC 1, Ch 3, 3DC in first Ch made, Ch 2, Slip stitch in first Ch made. Finish off.

Making the Spiral

Join with a single crochet at first stitch of row 2 and slip stitch around posts of each stitch in an upward spiral.

Horn

FOUNDATION: With DMC Ecru or White; Ch 2, SC 6 in second Ch from hook. 6
ROUND 1. 2SC around. 12
ROUND 2. SC in back loop only. 12
ROUND 3. 2SCtog, SC 10. 11
ROUND 4. 2SCtog, SC 9. 10
ROUND 5. 2SCtog, SC 8. 9
ROUND 6. 2SCtog, SC 7. 8
ROUND 7. 2SCtog, SC 6. 7
ROUND 8. 2SCtog, SC 5. 6
ROUND 9. 2SCtog, SC 4. 5
ROUND 10. 2SCtog, SC 3. 4
Stuff firmly, finish off in your preferred method.

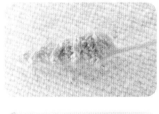

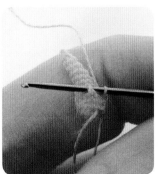

Assembly

STEP 1: Sew heart unto upper back, near tail.

STEP 2: Sew fins to either side of mid body.

STEP 3: Sew horn to upper center of head.

STEP 4: Use French knots or small beads to make eyes.

shortimer

Abbreviations

SC: Single Crochet

DC: Double Crochet

2SC: Single Crochet twice in same stitch

2SCTOG: Single Crochet two stitches together, or decrease

2DC: Double Crochet twice in same stitch

3SC: Single Crochet three times into same stitch

3SCTOG: Single Crochet three stitches together

SS: Slip Stitch

**: Repeat indicated directions across row

{}: Directions in brackets will be repeated a specified number of times

Materials

Skeins of DMC #225 for all of body,
Less than a skein of DMC #840 for feet, arms and detail embroidery
Size 10 crochet hook for double strand
Size 12 crochet hook for single strand
Small black beads for eyes (Optional)
Sewing needle

Head

FOUNDATION: With DMC #225; Ch 2, SC 6 in second Ch from hook. 6

ROUND 1. *2SC in each* around. 12

ROUND 2. *SC 1, 2SC in next* around. 18

ROUND 3. *SC 2, 2SC in next* around. 24

ROUND 4. *SC 3, 2SC in next* around. 30

ROUND 5. *SC 4, 2SC in next* around. 36

ROUND 6. *SC 5, 2SC in next* around. 42

ROUND 7. *SC 6, 2SC in next* around. 48

ROUNDS 8-10. SC around. 48

ROUND 11. SC 8, 2SC, SC 1, 2SC, SC 7, 2SC, SC 1, 2SC, SC 27. 52

ROUND 12. SC 8, 2SC, SC 15, 2SC, SC 27. 54

ROUND 13. SC 11, 2SC, SC 11, 2SC, SC 30. 56

ROUND 14. SC around. 56

ROUND 15. SC 7, {2SC} three times, SC 3, 2SC, SC 13, 2SC, SC 3, {2SC} three times, SC 22. 64

ROUND 16. SC 7, {SC 1, 2SC} three times, {2SCtog} twice, SC 10, {2SCtog} twice, {SC 1, 2SC} three times, SC 27. 66

ROUND 17. SC 16, 2SCtog, SC 10, 2SCtog, SC 36. 64

ROUND 18. *SC 6, 2SCtog* around. 56

ROUND 19. *SC 5, 2SCtog* around. 48

ROUND 20. *SC 2, 2SCtog* around. 36

ROUND 21. *SC 1, 2SCtog* around. 24

ROUND 22. *2SCtog* around. 12

ROUND 23. SC around. 12

ROUND 24. *2SCtog* around. 6

Finish off, stuff firmly while shaping snout.

Body

FOUNDATION: With DMC #225 Ch 2, SC 6 in second Ch from hook. 6

ROUND 1. *2SC in each* around. 12

ROUND 2. *SC 1, 2SC in next* around. 18

ROUND 3. *SC 2, 2SC in next* around. 24

ROUND 4. *SC 3, 2SC in next* around. 30

ROUND 5. *SC 4, 2SC in next* around. 36

ROUND 6. *SC 5, 2SC in next* around. 42

ROUNDS 7-9. SC around. 42

ROUND 10. *SC 5, 2SCtog* around. 36

ROUND 11. *SC 4, 2SCtog* around. 30

ROUNDS 12-13. SC around. 30

ROUND 14. *SC 3, 2SCtog* around. 24

ROUND 15. SC around. 24

ROUND 16. *SC 2, 2SCtog* around. 18

Finish off, stuff firmly.

Arms {Make 2}

FOUNDATION: Begin with DMC #840; Ch 2, SC 7 in second Ch from hook. 7

ROUND 1. {2SC} twice, 2DC, Ch 2, SS, Ch 2, 2DC, {2SC} twice. 15

ROUND 2. Work in back loop only; SC 6, 3SCtog, SC 6. 13

ROUND 3. Switch to DMC# 225; SC around. 13

ROUND 4. 2SCtog, SC 3, 2SCtog, SC 4, 2SCtog. 10

ROUND 5. SC around. 10

ROUND 6. 2SCtog, SC 2, 2SCtog, SC 2, 2SCtog. 7

Stuff tops only, finish off.

Tail

FOUNDATION: With DMC #225; Ch 2, SC 6 in second Ch from hook. 6

ROUND 1. {2SCtog} twice, SC 2. 4

ROUND 2. *2SCtog* around. 2

ROUND 3. Ch 8, SC loosely back down Ch starting in second Ch from hook. 7

Finish off with slip stitch to round 2.

Legs {Make 2}

FOUNDATION: Begin with DMC #840; Ch 2, SC 7 in second Ch from hook. 7

ROUND 1. *2SC in each* around. 14

ROUND 2. {SC 1, 2SC} twice, DC 1, 2DC, Ch 2, SS, Ch 2, 2DC, DC 1, {2SC, SC1} twice, 2SC. 25

ROUND 3. Work in back loop only; SC 9, 2SCtog, SC 1, 2SCtog, SC 11. 23

ROUND 4. 2SCtog, SC 7, 2SCtog, SC 10, 2SCtog. 20

ROUND 5. Switch to DMC #225; 2SCtog, SC 6, 2SCtog, SC 8, 2SCtog. 17

ROUND 6. SC 7, 2SCtog, SC 8. 16

ROUND 7. SC around. 17

ROUND 8. 2SCtog, SC 5, 2SCtog, SC 6, 2SCtog. 14

ROUND 9. 2SCtog, SC 3, 2SCtog, SC 4, 2SCtog. 11

ROUND 10. {2SCtog} five times, SC 1. 6

Stuff tops only, finish off.

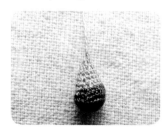

Ears {Make 2}

FOUNDATION: With DMC #225 Ch 7, turn. 7

ROUND 1. Begin in second Ch from hook; SC across, Ch 1, turn. 6

ROUND 2. SC across, Ch 1, turn. 6

ROUND 3. SC 1, DC 1, SC 2, DC 1, SC 1, Ch 2, turn. 6

ROUND 4. DC, HDC 1, 2SCtog, HDC 1, DC 1. 5

Finish off.

Snout

FOUNDATION: With DMC #225; Ch 7, 3SC in second Ch from hook, SC 4, 3SC in last Ch, turn piece and work in opposite side of Ch, SC 4. 14

ROUND 1. SC 3, SC 4 in back loop only, SC 7. 14

ROUND 2. SC 10, SC 4 in back loop only. 14

ROUNDS 3-4. SC around.

Finish off, stuff lightly.

Assembly

STEP 1: With DMC #225, run a loop through the head where you made the first and last set of extra stitches on rounds 11-16. Pull thread tight to make indents for eyes.

STEP 2: With DMC #840 add two small stitches on the front of snout to make nostrils.

STEP 3: Sew snout to lower face between indents for eyes.

STEP 4: Sew body to underside of head.

STEP 5: Sew legs to either side of lower body.

STEP 6: Sew arms to either side of upper body, keeping in line with the legs.

STEP 7: Sew tail to lower center of backside of body.

STEP 8: Sew ears to either side of upper head.

STEP 9: Use French knots or small beads to create eyes.

STEP 10: Embroider eyebrows with DMC #840.

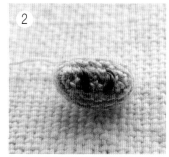

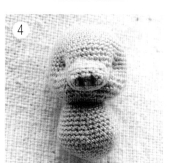

Paisley Peacock

Abbreviations

SC: Single Crochet

2SC: Single Crochet twice in same stitch

2SCTOG: Single Crochet two stitches together, or decrease

3SC: Single Crochet three times into same stitch

SS: Slip Stitch

**: Repeat indicated directions across row

{}: Directions in brackets will be repeated a specified number of times

Materials

Less than 1 skein of DMC #995 for all of body

Less than 1 skein of DMC #827 for wings and comb and outer tail feathers

Less than 1 skein of DMC #906 for tail feathers

Less than 1 skein of DMC #915 for tail feathers

Less than 1 skein of DMC black for beak

Size 10 crochet hook for double stranded

Size 12 crochet hook for single stranded

Small black beads or eyes {Optional}.

Sewing needle

Head and Body

FOUNDATION: Begin with DMC #995; Ch 2, SC 6 in second Ch from hook. 6

ROUND 1. *2SC in each* around. 12

ROUND 2. *SC 1, 2SC in next* around. 18

ROUND 3. *SC 2, 2SC in next* around. 24

ROUND 4. *SC 3, 2SC in next* around. 30

ROUND 5. {SC 4, 2SC in next} twice, SC 20. 32

ROUND 6. {SC 5, 2SC in next} twice, SC 20. 34

ROUND 7. {SC 6, 2SC in next} twice, SC 20. 36

ROUNDS 8-9. SC around. 36

ROUND 10. SC 16, {SC 3, 2SCtog} four times. 32

ROUND 11. *SC 2, 2SCtog* around. 24

ROUND 12. {2SCtog} nine times, SC 5. 15

ROUND 13. {2SCtog} four times, SC 6. 11

ROUNDS 14-16. SC around. 11

ROUND 17. SC 1, 2SC, SC 4, 2SC, SC 3. 13.

Stuff the head firmly here.

ROUND 18. SC 2, 2SC, SC 5, 2SC, SC 3. 15

ROUND 19. SC 3, 2SC, SC 6, {2SC} twice, SC 3. 18

ROUND 20. SC 4, 2SC, SC 6, {SC 1, 2SC in next} twice, SC 3. 21

ROUND 21. SC 5, 2SC, SC 6, {SC 2, 2SC in next} twice, SC 3. 24

ROUND 22. SC 6, 2SC, SC 6, {SC 3, 2SC in next} twice, SC 3. 27

Head, after stuffing.

ROUND 23. SC 7, 2SC, SC 5, {SC 1, 2SC} five times, SC 3. 33

ROUND 24. SC 8, 2SC, SC 5, {SC 2, 2SC} five times, SC 3. 39

ROUNDS 25-26. SC around. 39

ROUND 27. SC 16, {SC 3, 2SC} five times, SC 3. 44

ROUND 28. SC 16, {SC 4, 2SC} five times, SC 3. 49

ROUNDS 29-31. SC around. 49

ROUND 32. SC 16, {SC 4, 2SCtog} five times, SC 3. 44

ROUND 33. *SC 9, 2SCtog* around. 40

ROUND 34. *SC 8, 2SCtog* around. 36

ROUND 35. SC around. 36

ROUND 36. *SC 7, 2SCtog* around. 32

ROUND 37. *SC 6, 2SCtog* around. 28

ROUND 38. *SC 5, 2SCtog* around. 24

ROUND 39. *SC 4, 2SCtog* around. 20

ROUND 40. *SC 3, 2SCtog* around. 16

ROUND 41. *2SCtog* around. 8

Stuff remainder of body, finish off in your preferred method.

Comb

FOUNDATION: Begin with DMC #827, {Ch 5, SC 5 in second Ch from hook, Ch 1, SS in 3 remaining Chains} three times.

Finish off.

Wings

FOUNDATION: Begin with DMC #827; Ch 11, turn. 11

ROWS 1-4. Starting in second Ch from hook; SC across, Ch 1, turn. 10

ROW 5. 2SCtog, SC 6, 2SCtog, Ch 1, turn. 8

ROW 6. {Ch 4, Skip 1, SS 1} three times. 15

ROW 7. Working down edge of piece back toward first row; SC 7, Ch 1, Skip 1, 4DC, Skip 1, SS 1, Ch 1, Skip 1, 4DC, Ch 1, Skip 1, SC 6 along opposite edge. 25

ROW 8. SC 5 in each Ch 4 space. 15

Finish off

Beak

FOUNDATION: Begin with DMC Black; Ch 2, SC 6 in second Ch from hook. 6

ROUND 1. *2SC in each* around. 12

ROUND 2. SC in back loop only. 12

ROUND 3. {2SCtog} twice, SC 8. 10

ROUND 4. {2SCtog} twice, SC 6. 8

ROUND 5. {2SCtog} twice, SC 4. 6

ROUND 6. {2SCtog} three times. 3

Finish off .

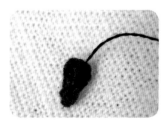

Tail Feather

Variation 1
{Make 1 or more}

FOUNDATION: Begin with DMC #906, Ch 2, SC 5 in second Ch from hook, Ch 1 turn. 5

ROUND 1. *2SC in each* across, Ch 1 turn. 10

ROUND 2. (Ch 9, Work feather bobble, SC 6 down foundation Ch, Skip 1, SS in next stitch of Row 1.) five times .

Finish off.

ROUND 3. Begin with DMC #915 and working only in the Ch 2 space of of each Feather Bobble; SC 1, 3DC, SC 1. 5

Finish off

ROUND 4. With DMC #827, Join with SC at corner of Feather Bobble, counts as first SC; *SC 5, 2SC in next, SC 5, Ch 1* across all feathers.

Feather Bobble

Work all in one stitch; Ch 2,
2DC in third Ch from hook,
Ch 2, 2DC in into third Ch,
Ch 2, SS into third Ch.

Variation 2
{Make 2 or more}

FOUNDATION: Begin with DMC
#906, Ch 2, SC 6 in second
Ch from hook, Ch 1 turn. 6

ROUND 1. *2SC in each*
across, Ch 1 turn. 12

ROUND 2. (Ch 9, Work
feather bobble, SC 6 down
foundation Ch , Skip 1, SS
in next stitch of Row 1.} six
times.
Finish off.

ROUND 3. Begin with DMC
#915 and working only in
the Ch 2 space of of each
Feather Bobble; SC 1, 3DC,
SC 1. 5
Finish off

ROUND 4. With DMC #827,
Join with SC at corner of
Feather Bobble, counts
as first SC. *SC 5, 2SC in
next, SC 5, Ch 3* across all
feathers.
Finish off.

Variation 3
{Make 2 or more}

FOUNDATION: Ch 2, SC 5 in
second Ch from hook, Ch 1
turn. 5

ROUND 1. *2SC in each*
across, Ch 1 turn. 10

ROUND 2. (Ch 14, Work
feather bobble, SC 11 down
foundation Ch , Skip 1, SS in
next stitch of Row 1.} five
times
Finish off.

ROUND 3. Begin with DMC
#915 and working only in
the Ch 2 space of of each
Feather Bobble; SC 1, 3DC,
SC 1. 5
Finish off

ROUND 4. With DMC #827;
Join with SC at corner of
Feather Bobble, counts
as first SC. *SC 5, 2SC in
next, SC 5, Ch 3* across all
feathers.
Finish off.

Variation 4
{Make 2 or more}

FOUNDATION: Ch 2, SC 6 in
second Ch from hook, Ch 1
turn. 6

ROUND 1. *2SC in each*
across, Ch 1 turn. 12

ROUND 2. (Ch 14, Work
feather bobble, SC 11 down
foundation Ch , Skip 1, SS
in next stitch of Row 1.} six
times
Finish off.

ROUND 3. Begin with DMC
#915 and working only in
the Ch 2 space of of each
Feather Bobble; SC 1, 3DC,
SC 1. 5
Finish off

ROUND 4. With DMC #827,
Join with SC at corner of
Feather Bobble, counts
as first SC; *SC 5, 2SC in
next, SC 5, Ch 3* across all
feathers.
Finish off.

Variation 5
{Make 1}

FOUNDATION: Ch 2, SC 5 in
second Ch from hook, Ch 1
turn. 5

ROUND 1. *2SC in each*
across, Ch 1 turn. 10

ROUND 2. (Ch 14, Work
feather bobble, SC 1 down
foundation Ch, Skip 1, SS in
next stitch of Row 1.} five
times.
Finish off.

ROUND 3. Begin with DMC
#915 and working only in
the Ch 2 space of of each
Feather Bobble; SC 1, 3DC,
SC 1. 5
Finish off

ROUND 4. With DMC #827,
Join with SC at corner of
Feather Bobble, counts
as first SC; *SC 5, 2SC in
next, SC 5, Ch 3* across all
feathers.
Finish off.

Assembly

STEP 1: Sew comb to center of head.

STEP 2: Sew the beak in the lower middle of face.

STEP 3: Sew wings to either side of body, going only three quarters around and leaving the feathered end open.

STEP 4: Sew Tail feathers together in a stack starting with Variation 1 and ending with Variation 5.

STEP 5: Once you've arranged your tail feathers to your liking, sew the stack onto the upper center of backside.

STEP 6: Use French knots to make eyes.

STEP 7: Embroider some eyebrows.

1

2
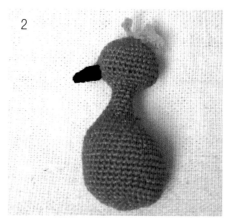

3

4
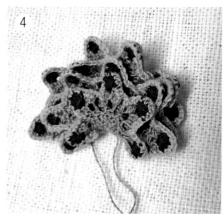

5

6

7

Ruby

Abbreviations

SC: Single Crochet

2SC: Single Crochet twice in same stitch

2SCTOG: Single Crochet two stitches together, or decrease

2DC: Double Crochet twice in same stitch

HDC: Half Double Crochet

3SC: Single Crochet three times into same stitch

SS: Slip Stitch

**: Repeat indicated directions across row

{}: Directions in brackets will be repeated a specified number of times

Materials

Skein of DMC #919 for body, tail and face.

Skein of DMC #801 for legs and tail

Skein of DMC #822 for face and tail

Size 10 crochet hook for double stand

Size 12 crochet hook for single strand.

Small to medium black beads for eyes.**

Sewing needle

**Optional

Head

FOUNDATION: With DMC #822; Ch 2, SC 6 in second Ch from hook. 6

ROUND 1. *2SC in each* around. 12

ROUND 2. *SC 1, 2SC in next* around. 18

ROUND 3. *SC 2, 2SC in next* around. 24

ROUND 4. SC around. 24

ROUND 5. *SC 3, 2SC in next* around. 30

ROUND 6. *SC 4, 2SC in next* around. 36

ROUND 7. *SC 5, 2SC in next8 around. 42

ROUNDS 8-10. SC around. 42

ROUND 11. *SC 5, 2SCtog* around. 36

ROUND 12. SC around. 36

ROUND 13. *SC 4, 2SCtog* around. 30

ROUND 14. *SC 3, 2SCtog* around. 24

ROUND 15. *SC 2, 2SCtog* around. 18

ROUND 16. *2SCtog* around. 9

Stuff firmly, finish off in your preferred method and squish a bit flat.

Body

FOUNDATION: With DMC #3033; Ch 2, SC 6 in second Ch from hook. 6
ROUND 1. *2SC in each* around. 12
ROUND 2. *SC 1, 2SC in next* around. 18
ROUND 3. *SC 2, 2SC in next* around. 24
ROUND 4. *SC 3, 2SC in next* around. 30
ROUNDS 5-6. SC around. 30
ROUND 6. *SC 4, 2SC in next* around. 36
ROUNDS 7-10. SC around. 36
ROUND 11. *SC 4, 2SCtog* around. 30
ROUND S 12-18. SC around. 30
ROUND 19. *SC 3, 2SCtog* around. 24
ROUND 20. SC around. 24
ROUND 21. *SC 2, 2SCtog* around. 18
Finish off, stuff medium firm and squish a bit flat.

Front Legs {Make 2}

FOUNDATION: With DMC #801; Ch 2, SC 5 in second Ch from hook. 5
ROUND 1. *2SC in each* around. 10
ROUND 2. *SC 1, 2SC in next* around. 15
ROUND 3. {SC 1, 2SCtog} three times, SC 6. 12
ROUND 4. SC 1, 2SCtog, SC 9. 11
ROUND 5. SC 4 in front loop only, SC 7 in both. 11
ROUND S 6-7. SC around. 11

Back Legs {Make 2}

FOUNDATION: With DMC #801; Ch 2, SC 5 in second Ch from hook. 5
ROUND 1. *2SC in each* around. 10
ROUND 2. *SC 1, 2SC in next* around. 15
ROUND 3. {SC 1, 2SCtog} twice, SC 9. 13
ROUND 4. SC 4 in front loop only, SC 9 in both loops. 13
ROUND 5. SC 6, 2SCtog, SC 5. 12
ROUND 6-7. SC around. 12

Snout

FOUNDATION: With DMC #822; Ch 2, SC 6 in second Ch from hook. 6

ROUND 1. {2SC} four times, SC 2. 10

ROUND 2. {SC 1, 2SC} four times, SC 2. 14

ROUND 3. {SC 2, 2SC} four times, SC 2. 18

Right Eye Piece

FOUNDATION: With DMC #822; Ch 5, turn. 5

ROUND 1. 2DC in second from hook, SC 1, SS. 5 (first two chains count as one stitch)

Finish off.

Left Eye Piece

FOUNDATION: With DMC #822; Ch 5, turn. 5

ROW 1. SS, SC 1, 2DC, DC

Finish off.

Right Outer Ear

FOUNDATION: With DMC #822; Ch 2, SC 5 in second Ch from hook, Ch 1 turn. 5

ROUND 1. 2SC, SC 2, {2SC} twice., Ch 1, turn. 8

ROUND 2. 3SC, 2SC, SC 3, 2SC, SC 2, Ch 1, turn. 12

ROUND 3. 2SCtog, SC 1, 3SC, 2SC, SC 1, 2SCtog, SC 1, 3SC, SC 2, Ch 1, turn. 16

Finish off.

Left Outer Ear

FOUNDATION: Ch 2, SC 5 in second Ch from hook, Ch 1 turn. 5

ROUND 1. {2SC} twice, SC 2, 2SC, Ch 1, turn. 8

ROUND 2. SC 2, 2SC, SC 3, 2SC, 3SC, Ch 1, turn. 12

ROUND 3. SC 2, 3SC, SC 1, 2SCtog, SC 1, 2SC, 3SC, SC 1, 2SCtog, Ch 1, turn. 16

Finish off.

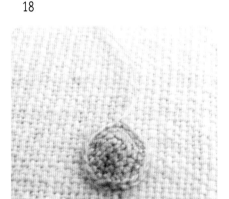

Inner Ear {Make 2}

FOUNDATION: With DMC #822; Ch 2, SC 4 in second ch from hook, Ch 1 turn. 4

ROUND 1. 2SC, SC 2, 3SC. 7

Finish off.

Right Cheek Piece

FOUNDATION: Ch 7, turn. 7

ROUND 1. SC in second Ch from hook, HDC 2, DC 2, SC 1. 7

Finish off.

Left Cheek Piece

FOUNDATION: With DMC# 822; Ch 5, turn. 5

ROUND 1. SS, SC 1, 2DC, DC.

Finish off.

Tail

FOUNDATION: Ch 2, SC 6 in second loop from hook. 6

ROUND 1. *2SC in each* around. 12

ROUND 2. *SC 1, 2SC in next* around. 18

ROUND 3. {SC 2, 2SC} three times, SC 9. 21

ROUND 4. SC around. 21

ROUND 5. Switch to DMC #; {SC 2, 2SC} three times, SC 9. 18

ROUND 6. Switch to DMC#; SC around. 18

ROUND S 7-8. Switch to DMC #; SC around. 18

ROUND 9. Switch to DMC #; SC around. 18

ROUND 10. Switch to DMC #; 2SCtog, SC 16. 17

ROUND 11. SC around. 20

ROUND 12. Switch to DMC #; 2SCtog, SC 15. 16

ROUND 13. Switch to DMC #; *SC 2, 2SCtog* around. 12

ROUND 14. SC around. 12

ROUND 15. Switch to DMC #; SC around. 12

ROUND 16. Switch to DMC #; *SC 1, 2SCtog* around. 8

ROUND 17. SC around.

Finish off, Stuff medium firm.

Assembly

STEP 1: Sew body to head on the wider side made by squishing.

STEP 2: Sew front legs to either side of body right under join between head and body.

STEP 3: Sew back legs to either side of body at the back end.

STEP 4: Sew inner ear piece to each of the outer ear pieces.

STEP 5: Take finished ear and fold tip just enough to give it a curve and sew in place on either side of the upper head.

STEP 6: Embroider nose and sew snout into place, do not stuff.

STEP 7: Sew eye pieces above snout and part way between snout and ears.

STEP 8: Sew cheek pieces slightly under and just outside of eye pieces.

STEP 9: Sew tail to back side, just up from center and curve tail downward.

STEP 10: Add French knots or small beads for eyes.

sheldon

Abbreviations

SC: Single Crochet
2SC: Single Crochet twice in same stitch
2SCTOG: Single Crochet two stitches together, or decrease
**: Repeat indicated directions across row
{}: Directions in brackets will be repeated a specified number of times

Materials

Less than 1 skein of DMC# 3033 for body
Less than 1 skein color of your choice for shells.
Size 10 crochet hook for double strand.
Size 12 crochet hook for single strand.
Small to medium black beads for eyes.**
Sewing needle

**Optional

Body

FOUNDATION: With DMC #3033; Ch 2, SC 6 in second Ch from hook. 6
ROUND 1. *2SC in each* around. 12
ROUND 2. *SC 1, 2SC in next* around. 18
ROUNDS 3-4. SC around. 18
ROUND 5. *SC 1, 2SCtog* around. 12
ROUND 6. *2SCtog* around. 6
ROUND 7. *2SC in each* around. 12
Stuff head firmly here.
ROUNDS 8-17. SC around. 12
ROUND 18. 2SCtog, SC 10. 11
ROUND 19. 2SCtog, SC 9. 10
ROUND 20. 2SCtog, SC 8. 9.
ROUND 21. *SC 1, 2SCtog* around. 6
Finish off in your preferred method.

Body Edging

JWSC to end of snail body, keeping it folded flat, work along the edge. *SC 1, 2SC* until you reach row 8. At row 8, fold head back toward body and begin working around the posts of row 8 and 9. *SC 1, 2SC* until you reach the edge, then resume working along side of snail. *SC 1, 2SC*. The exact number of stitches on this step is not crucial and adds variation to the finished snails.

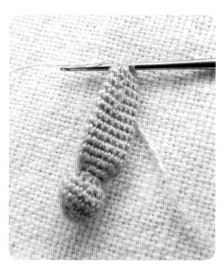

Shell

FOUNDATION: With DMC color of your choice; Ch 2, SC 6 in second Ch from hook. 6

ROUND 1. *2SC in each* around. 12

ROUNDS 2-22 SC around. 12

Finish off, do not stuff.

Optional; Give your shell some decorative patterning with French knots or back stitches.

Assembly

STEP 1: Thread a needle with one strand, run it through the upper center of head to create antennae. Cut thread close to head, you can use some fabric glue to help shape and hold the antennae, but it isn't necessary if it won't be handled.

STEP 2: Coil shell into a spiral shape. Sew into place.

STEP 3: If you are going to add decorative stitches to your snail's shell do so now.

STEP 4: Sew Shell to Snail body.

STEP 5: Use French knots or very small beads to create eyes.

STEP 6: Embroider eyebrows.

If you leave the shell off altogether you have yourself a tiny little slug.

Tara N. Tula

Abbreviations

SC: Single Crochet
2SC: Single Crochet twice in same stitch
2SCTOG: Single Crochet two stitches together, or decrease
**: Repeat indicated directions across row
{}: Directions in brackets will be repeated a specified number of times

**Optional

Materials

Skein of any colored floss you like, spiders do come in an array of colors
Skein of any darker or red color for eyes
Size 10 crochet hook for double stand
Size 12 crochet hook for single strand.
Small to medium black beads for eyes.**
Sewing needle

Body

FOUNDATION: With DMC color of your choice; Ch 2, SC 6 in second Ch from hook. 6

ROUND 1. *2SC in each* around. 12

ROUND 2. *SC 1, 2SC in next* around. 18

ROUND 3. *SC 2, 2SC in next* around. 24

ROUND 4. *SC 3, 2SC in next* around. 30

ROUND 5. *SC 4, 2SC in next* around. 36

ROUNDS 6-8. SC around. 36

ROUND 9. *SC 10, 2SCtog* around. 33

ROUND 10. *SC 9, 2SCtog* around. 30

ROUNDS 11-12. SC around. 30

ROUND 13. *SC 8, 2SCtog* around. 27

ROUND 14. *SC 7, 2SCtog* around. 24

ROUND 15. *SC 6, 2SCtog* around. 21

ROUND 16. *SC 5, 2SCtog* around. 18

ROUND 17. *SC 4, 2SCtog* around. 15

ROUND 18. *SC 3, 2SCtog* around. 12

Finish off, stuff firmly and shape the bottom to be flat.

Head

FOUNDATION: Ch 2, SC 6 in second Ch from hook. 6

ROUND 1. *2SC in each* across. 12

ROUND 2. *SC 1, 2SC in next* around. 18

ROUND 3. *SC 2, 2SC innext* around. 24

ROUNDS 4-7. SC around. 24

ROUND 8. *2SCtog* around. 12

ROUND 9. SC around. 12

ROUND 10. *2SCtog* around. 6

Stuff firmly, finish off in your preferred method

Legs {Method One}

Cut four pieces of thin wire. The length will depend on how long you want the spider's legs to be, but it needs to be double the length of one leg plus the width of the body.

Insert pieces of wire into the body near the flattened bottom at evenly spaced intervals.

Single Crochet around the wire, slide stitch almost to end of wire. Bend back end of wire and pinch closed. SC around wire up the leg. The amount of stitches you use will depend on the length of your leg, but you'll want to make sure the wire is completely covered.

Finish off, leave a long tail to anchor crocheted portion of leg to the body.

Legs {Method Two}

Make a Chain the length you'd like your finished legs to be, add one stitch and turn. Begin in second Ch from hook and SC across, Ch 1, turn. Repeat for a total of three rows, finish off.

Take finished pieced and sew edges together lengthwise. Make 8.

Assembly

STEP 1: Sew head to opening of body

STEP 2: If using leg method one, work now.

STEP 3: If using leg method two, sew legs to body near flattened bottom at evenly spaced intervals.

STEP 4: Use larger French knots or medium sized beads to add first set of eyes on either side of center of head.

STEP 5: Use smaller French knots or small beads to add a second set of eyes just outside and above the first set.

STEP 6: Optional: With white embroider on some fangs

Drake

ROUND 2. *SC 1, 2SC in next* around. 18

ROUND 3. *SC 2, 2SC in next* around. 24

ROUND 4. *SC 3, 2SC in next* around. 30

ROUND 5. *SC 4, 2SC in next* around. 36

ROUND 6. *SC 5, 2SC in next* around. 42

ROUNDS 7-8. SC around. 42

ROUND 9. SC 2, {2SC} four times, SC 7, {2SC} four times, SC 25. 50

ROUND 10. SC 4, {2SC} four times, SC 11, {2SC} four times, SC 27. 58

ROUNDS 11-15. SC around 58

ROUND 16. SC 12, 2SCtog, SC 5, 2SCtog, SC 36. 56

ROUND 17. *SC 5, 2SCtog* around. 48

ROUND 18. *SC 4, 2SCtog* around. 40

ROUND 19. *SC 3, 2SCtog* around. 32

ROUND 20. SC around. 32

ROUND 21. *SC 2, 2SCtog* around. 24

ROUND 22. *SC 1, 2SCtog* around. 16

ROUNDS 23-24. SC around. 16

ROUND 25. *2SC in each* around . 32

ROUND 26-27. SC around. 32

Abbreviations

SC: Single Crochet

2SC: Single Crochet twice in same stitch

2SCTOG: Single Crochet two stitches together, or decrease

JWSC: Join with Single Crochet

**: Repeat indicated directions across row

{}: Directions in brackets will be repeated a specified number of times

Materials

1 Skein of DMC #307 for body and wings

Less than 1 skein DMC# 743

Size 10 crochet hook for double stand

Size 12 crochet hook for single strand.

Small to medium black beads for eyes.**

Sewing needle

**Optional

Head and Body

FOUNDATION: With DMC #307; Ch 2, SC 6 in second Ch from hook. 6

ROUND 1. *2SC in each* around. 12

Stuff head firmly here.

ROUND 28. {SC 1, 2SC} four times, SC 16, {SC 1, 2SC} four times. 40

ROUND 29. SC around. 40

ROUND 30. {SC 2, 2SC} four times, SC 16, {SC 2, 2SC } four times. 48

ROUNDS 31-36. SC around. 48

ROUND 37. {2SC} twice, SC 44, {2SC} twice. 52

ROUND 38. {2SC} twice, SC 48, {2SC} twice. 56

ROUND 39. SC 6, 2SCtog, {SC 2, 2SCtog} three times, SC 16, 2SCtog, {SC 2, 2SCtog} three times, SC 6. 48

ROUND 40. SC 7, {SC 1, 2SCtog} three times, SC 17, {SC 1, 2SCtog} three times, SC 6. 42

ROUND 41. SC 5, {2SCtog} four times, SC 17, {2SCtog} four times, SC 4. 34

ROUND 42. SC 4, {SC 2,

2SCtog} six times, SC 1, Ch 12, Skip last four stitches of round and first four of what would be the next round, {2SCtog} twice. This will be your new end points for remaining rows. 33

ROUND 43. *SC 1, 2SCtog* around. 22

ROUND 44. *2SCtog* around. 1 Stuff firmly and finish off in your preferred method.

Feet

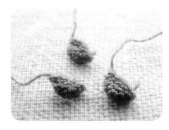

Web Tips {Make 6}

FOUNDATION: With DMC #743; Ch 2, SC 5 in second Ch from hook. 5

ROUND 1. *2SC in each* around. 10

ROUND 2. SC around. 10 Finish off.

Joining Feet Together

FOUNDATION: With DMC #743; Join three web tips together with on SC each.

ROUND 1. JWSC and then SC around joined web tips. 26

ROUND 2. {SC 7, 2SCtog} twice, SC 8. 24

ROUND 3. *SC 6, 2SCtog* around. 21

ROUND 4. *SC 5, 2SCtog* around. 18

ROUND 5. *SC 4, 2SCtog* around. 15

ROUNDS 6-7. SC around. 15

ROUND 8. *SC 3, 2SCtog* around. 12

ROUND 9. *2SCtog* around. 6 Very lightly stuff, while keeping piece fairly flat. Finish off in your preferred method.

Wings {Make 2}

FOUNDATION: With DMC #307; Ch 2, SC 7 in second Ch from hook. 7

ROUND 1. SC around. 7

ROUND 2. {2SC} four times, SC 3. 11

ROUND 3. SC around. 11

ROUND 4. SC 4, {2SC} twice, SC 5. 13

ROUNDS 5-6. SC around. 13 Finish off.

Bill

FOUNDATION: With DMC #740; Ch 11, turn. 11

ROUND 1. Begin in second Ch from hook; 4SC, SC 8, 4SC in last Chain, turn piece and work up opposite side of Chain, SC 8. 24

ROUND 2. SC 1, {2SC} twice, SC 10, {2SC} twice, SC 9. 28

ROUNDS 3-6. SC around. 28

ROUND 7. SC 10, {2SC} four times, SC 12, {2SC} four times, SC 2. 36

ROUNDS 8-11. SC around. 36 Stuff lightly, keeping flat. Finish off.

Assembly

STEP 1: Sew opening made on bottom of body closed with the top part sticking out enough to form a tail.

STEP 2: Sew bill to lower center of face.

STEP 3: Sew feet to bottom of body.

STEP 4: Sew wings to either sider of upper body.

STEP 5: Use smaller French knots or small beads to add eyes above and outside the bill.

STEP 6: Embroider eyebrows.

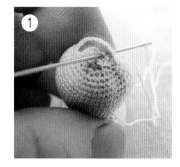
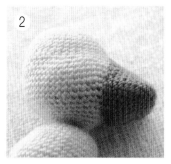
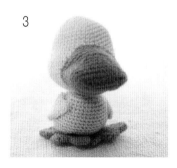

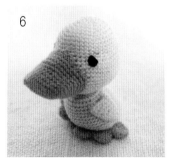